The Gardening Yearbook

Photography
John Glover Photography
Neil Sutherland

Design
Paul Turner and Sue Pressley

Editorial
Compiled and written by David Squire

Typesetting
DSP, Maidstone, Kent

Line artwork
John Hutchinson

Jacket
Photography: John Glover Photography

Production
Ruth Arthur
Sally Connolly

Director of production
Gerald Hughes

CLB 3192
This edition printed in 1994
© 1993 Colour Library Books Ltd, Godalming, Surrey
All rights reserved
Printed and bound in Italy by New Interlitho
ISBN 1-85833-030-0

The Gardening Yearbook

Compiled and written by David Squire

Colour Library Books

Introduction

Gardening is such an all-embracing hobby that reminders about what to do throughout the year are always welcome. Here, for every week of the year, there are ideas about what to do, such as in flower gardens or on a patio, creating and improving lawns, growing vegetables, producing fruit and growing plants in greenhouses.

Because gardeners usually want to personalise their garden, making it different from and better than any other, it is necessary to make notes about varieties, planting schemes and ways to improve the garden next year. Therefore, in this book there is space to make notes on each day of the year.

Few hobbies are so influenced by the capricious nature of our weather as gardening. Late spring frosts, summer storms, high winds in autumn and sub-zero conditions in winter may cause annoyance but they seldom deter us from gardening.

There is also a weather pattern peculiar to your own garden. Bands of hills, proximity to the Gulf Stream, a southerly or northerly aspect and trees forming a shelter belt all influence local weather, and although frosts may occur in some northerly areas until as late as the first week in June, in the southwest they may be unheard of throughout most of the winter. Therefore, it is necessary to understand your local weather pattern and to keep a few notes about it in this book. This information will better enable you to judge when to plant out frost-tender, summer-flowering bedding plants, put hanging-baskets outside on patios, prune roses, move late-flowering chrysanthemums into greenhouses in autumn, and so on.

Wild flower gardens are popular and a range of native plants to create these areas is suggested on pages 152 and 153. They create bright, natural areas attractive to insects and birds, and some plants specifically attract butterflies and bees.

Encouraging birds into gardens is important and specific foods to attract them are also suggested.

To enable you to create a directory of gardening services, there is space at the back of this book for telephone numbers of local gardening services, such as garden centres, nurseries, fencing contractors, landscapes designers, turfing services and tool hire shops. Once entered in this book, they will save you having repeatedly to search through directories, scraps of paper and old diaries.

This is not a diary just for one year, but a storehouse of general and personalised gardening information that can be added to from year to year.

January

January storms of wind and rain
Bring the bitter ice and snow
Yet even while the frosts remain
Under the trees the snowdrops glow

January

1

Seeds to sow this month are suggested throughout these pages

2

3

4

Don't use ashes or salt to clear cottage-garden paths of snow or ice as this damages plants set in crevices between the slabs.

5

6

Avoid treading on gardens unnecessarily when they are covered with snow. Lawn edges and plants can soon become broken.

7

There is usually a garden society in your area which will provide useful advice about local soils and weather. Also, some societies offer garden materials and equipment at reduced costs.

Flowers

Make a note of areas in flower beds - as well as throughout the rest of the garden - that retain water. These may need to have rubble or tile drains installed when the weather allows.

Flowers

Gently remove snow from plants. If left, it weighs them down, sometimes breaking branches. Use a pole or piece of tubular plastic to tap and scrape it away. Clumps of bamboos are especially badly damaged by snow and unless quickly removed it bends canes at ground level.

Sweet Williams

Organic Gardening

When growing food for the home, select varieties that appeal to your family. Too often, varieties offered in shops are those that commercially are the easiest and most profitable to grow, last well while being transported and are eye-catching on shelves.

Lawns

Arrange to have the cutting blades on your lawn mower sharpened. Alternatively, sharpen the blades of hover-mowers yourself and check the cutting ability of cylinder-mowers by passing a piece of paper between the blades. Have all electric cables and switching gear checked. Fit safety devices that instantly turn off the power if cables are damaged.

Fruit

When the weather allows, spray fruit trees with a tar-oil winter wash to kill overwintering eggs of pests. Thoroughly soak the trees. This also helps to remove algae.

Greenhouses

Water plants carefully in winter when they are not growing rapidly. If excessively watered, they wilt and their roots rot.

Plants from seeds

Most garden flowers raised from seeds are listed as herbaceous perennials, hardy annuals, half-hardy annuals or biennials. Although this gives an indication of the way they are increased, a few do not easily fit into these classifications.
For example:

❀ Snapdragons (*Antirrhinum majus*) are short-lived, woody perennials grown either as half-hardy annuals or hardy annuals.

❀ Alyssum (*Alyssum maritimum*, but now known as *Lobularia maritima*) is an annual usually grown as a half-hardy annual, but also as a hardy annual.

❀ Lobelia (*Lobelia erinus*) is a half-hardy perennial grown as a half-hardy annual.

❀ Busy Lizzie (*Impatiens sultanii*) is a greenhouse perennial grown as a half-hardy annual.

❀ Daisies (*Bellis perennis*) and Sweet Williams (*Dianthus barbatus*) are hardy perennials grown as biennials.

The sowing instructions recommended throughout this book are ways to increase plants and do not necessarily indicate a plant's normal nature.

Busy Lizzie, a greenhouse perennial invariably grown as a long-lasting half-hardy annual, creates colour throughout summer. It is important to keep these plants watered during dry weather.

January

8

9

Put both plastic and clay pots under cover. Plastic pots become brittle, while clay ones often crack when frozen.

10

11

This is often a month of reflection and looking forward to another season. Send away for seed and plant catalogues.

12

13

14

Check greenhouse doors and ventilators to ensure they fit properly. And have a few spare panes of glass in case of damage. Temporary repairs can be made with a piece of plastic sheeting - or a carrier-bag - secured in place to timber-framed greenhouses with wooden battens and nails.

Ponds frequently become frozen, preventing fish gaining vital oxygen. Also, gases expelled by decaying vegetable material in the water become trapped under the ice. To free an area of ice, place a kettle of boiling water on the surface. Depending on the thickness of the ice, the treatment may have to be repeated. Take care not to let the kettle fall through the ice! Do not make a hole by hitting the ice, as this cause shock waves that may kill fish.

Flowers
Begin planning flower borders - both spring and summer-flowering bedding types as well as those for herbaceous plants. Sketch out the border's outline on graph paper, select plants and order them from seed companies and nurseries.

Greenhouses
Prepare for starting chrysanthemum stools (roots and woody bases) into growth to produce cuttings that will root and develop into plants for flowering later in the year. Initially, ensure a supply of clean boxes, loam-based potting compost and labels.

Vegetables

Sow early cauliflowers in gentle warmth in a greenhouse to produce plants for planting in a vegetable plot in March or April. ▼

Organic Gardening

When creating a compost heap, beware of attracting rats and other vermin when putting out kitchen scraps, especially in winter. Use a wire-framed compost heap with a meshed top, or a proprietary type with a hinged lid.

Plants from seeds

❀ Herbaceous perennials die down to soil-level in autumn and send up fresh shoots in spring.

❀ Annuals grow from seeds, flower and die within the same year.

❀ Hardy annuals are sown outside in their flowering places.

❀ Half-hardy annuals are raised in gentle warmth early in the year and planted outside as soon as the risk of severe frost has passed. They then flower and die within the same year.

❀ Biennials are sown one year and flower during the following one. Seeds are sown in a seedbed, germinate, and the young plants are transferred to a nurserybed. In autumn - or early the following year - they are planted into their flowering positions.

Chrysanthemum 'Rylite' is ideal in flower arrangements, as well as in gardens.

Right: Godetia 'Sybil Sherwood' (bottom) and Coreopsis 'Special Mixture'.

15

16

17

18

When planning your garden, do not give tender plants an east-facing position. In winter, early-morning sun rapidly thaws frozen plants and damages them.

19

20

21

Some birds are beneficial to gardeners, eating grubs as well as small rodents. In winter, when natural food is scarce, they need to have their diet supplemented by gardeners (see pages 152 and 153 for details).

Flowers

Prepare the ground for dahlias, which are gross feeders and benefit from plenty of farmyard manure and compost. As well as providing plant foods, it helps to retain moisture in the soil.

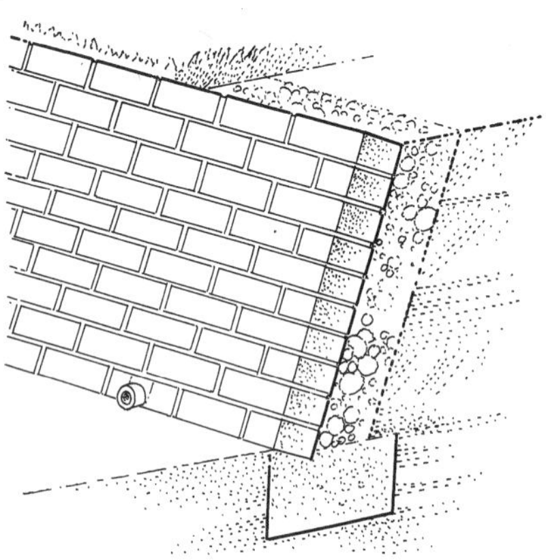

When constructing a retaining wall, make the foundations strong and slightly slope the brickwork backwards (often called battered). Fill the space behind the wall with 30cm/12in of rubble. Also, every 1.5m/5ft along the wall's base insert pipes to enable water to escape.

Vegetables

Harvest winter cabbages as they mature.

From the end of July to the first frosts of autumn, dahlias create a riot of exciting colours.

Flowers grown as half-hardy annuals to sow this month in gentle warmth in a greenhouse

- ❀ Lobelia
  (*Lobelia erinus*)
- ❀ Petunia
  (*Petunia x hybrida*)
- ❀ Salvia
  (*Salvia patens*)
- ❀ Salvia
  (*Salvia splendens*)

Organic Gardening

Take care in winter when creating a bonfire not to incinerate hibernating animals. Don't just put a match to a pile of rubbish: instead, build a fresh heap several yards away, moving small amounts one at a time from the existing heap.

Petunias, superbly coloured annuals, are ideal in both hanging baskets and flower borders.

Fruit

Prune apple trees. Burn the prunings to prevent the spread of pests and diseases.

Greenhouses

Sow tomato seeds to produce plants for growing in greenhouses. Space the seeds about 2.5cm/1in apart, sowing them 6mm/¼in deep. Place them in 16℃/61℉ and cover with a piece of glass. Invert the glass every day to prevent moisture falling on the compost, and remove as soon as the seeds germinate. ▼

January

22

23

When the north wind do blow,
We shall have snow.

24

25

Order seeds to avoid disappointment
later.

26

27

28

Construct and repair fences when the soil
can be walked on - not when frozen,
waterlogged or covered with snow. If this
job is left until spring, emerging bulbs
may be trodden on. Also, leaves and
stems obscure boundaries in spring and
summer. Additionally, it is easier to
knock stakes into damp soil than during
summer, when it may be dry and hard.

Flowers
Check dahlia tubers in store to ensure
they are not wet and decaying.

Flowers
Ensure chrysanthemum stools (cut down
plants) that were lifted in autumn and
packed in boxes with loam-based
compost around them have survived the
winter in a cold but frost-proof shed.

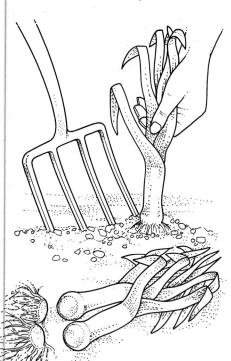

Vegetables
Continue to harvest leeks, trimming the
roots and removing soil.

Vegetables
When harvesting trench celery, use a
trowel to move soil from around plants,
then a garden fork to ease them out of
the ground.

Fruit
If not completed, spray fruit trees with a
tar-oil winter wash. Ensure the spraying
equipment is thoroughly cleaned after
use, then store it in a dry shed.

Organic Gardening

Check fruit trees to ensure all
fruits from the previous year have
been picked. If left on a tree, they
encourage the presence of pests
and diseases.

Left: Cyclamen are superb houseplants.

Below: Calceolarias are superb houseplants.

Fruit

Cut off sucker-like shoots from around
the bases and stems of apple and pear
trees. If they arise from the trunk, use a
sharp knife to severe them flush with the
bark. When growing from below ground
level, remove soil and cut the shoot close
to its point of origin.

Greenhouses

Sow cyclamen seeds for flowering during
the following winter. Space out the
seeds, using the point of a pencil or
knife, and cover with 6mm/¼in of
compost. Place in 13-16°C/55-61°F.

Greenhouses

The branches of trees and shrubs often
encroach upon greenhouses, blocking
out light. Cut off branches shading south
sides, but leave trees on northerly and
easterly aspects to create windbreaks
from cold winds.

*Above: Richly coloured antirrhinums are
available in a wide range of colours and heights.*

January

29

Lift parsnips, using a garden fork to ease them out of the soil.

30

Order seeds now for sowing in spring.

31

Order seed potatoes to avoid disappointment later.

If you have a spare piece of land - or wish to reduce the amount of formal garden - consider creating a wild-flower garden. Many seed companies offer wild flowers, singly or in mixtures, and include Cowslips, Wild Primroses, Poppies, Corn Marigolds, Knapweed, Wild Pansies, Field Scabious, Wild Cornflowers and Feverfew. ▼

Flowers

Major changes to gardens are best undertaken during winter and until early spring, but not if the soil if frozen, waterlogged or covered in snow.

▲
Patio surfaces and paths, especially when in shade and with badly-drained surfaces, become covered with algae. Either remove it with copious amounts of water and a stiff brush, or spray with a tar-oil winter wash.

Greenhouses

Check the staging to ensure it is secure. Water, humidity and strong sunlight throughout the year causes wood to deteriorate rapidly. Replace decayed wood and paint with an environmentally-friendly wood preservative.

Greenhouses

If you have been growing tomatoes directly in border soil in a greenhouse - and their yield has slowly declined - dig out the soil and replace with fresh compost. Alternatively, grow plants in pots or growing-bags placed on the border soil.

Greenhouses

When buying houseplants, ensure they are wrapped before leaving the nursery or garden centre - and get them home rapidly. Do not buy houseplants that are displayed outdoors - they may not immediately show signs of distress, but later flower buds fall off and the plant collapses.

Streptocarpus x hybridus 'Lisa'. Other varieties in white, rose to blue and purple.

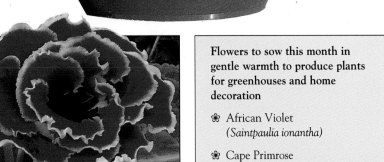

An African Violet makes a perfect present.

Organic Gardening

When selecting varieties of vegetables and fruits, choose those that are resistant to diseases and cultural problems. For instance, some vegetables are resistant to 'bolting' (the premature development of flowering shoots and flowers), while others have a degree of resistance to rusts, mildew and viruses. Also, some vegetable varieties store better than others. Consult seed catalogues.

Gloxinias need warmth and shade, as well as compost that is kept evenly moist.

Flowers to sow this month in gentle warmth to produce plants for greenhouses and home decoration

- ❀ African Violet
  (*Saintpaulia ionantha*)

- ❀ Cape Primrose
  (*Streptocarpus x hybridus*)

- ❀ Cyclamen
  (*Cyclamen persicum*)

- ❀ Gloxinia
  (*Sinningia speciosa*)

- ❀ Temple Bells
  (*Smithiantha hybrida*)

February

Now crocuses come smiling through
Grey February's fog and mist
Gold like the sun, deep lilac too
Defying winter's icy kiss

February

1

Sow seeds of greenhouse plants and houseplants, as indicated for this month.

2

3

4

As the outside temperature rises, increasingly open the ventilators on the leeside of your greenhouse. Avoid creating draughts.

5

6

7

Late winter is a time to review gardens and decide about further plants, perhaps a border packed with winter-flowering shrubs or one bursting with spring-flowering bulbs. These two features can be combined - bulbs grow well under deciduous shrubs, where they receive slight protection from frost in winter and have good light in spring.

Flowers ▲

In mild areas, where the risk of further severe frost is not high, prune the Butterfly Bush (*Buddleia davidii*). Cut all the previous season's shoots back to within 5-7.5cm/2-3in of the old wood. This severe pruning encourages the development of strong shoots that will bear flowers during July and August.

Flowers

Gaps in beds of Wallflowers can be filled by forking up and replanting a few of those planted around shrubs - or from spare plants earlier heeled-in in a nursery-bed. Also, re-firm plants loosened by the action of frost.

Lawns ▲

Where stepping stones in lawns have settled below the surface, lift them and place sand underneath. Use a straight-edged board to check their height - flush with the surface of the lawn.

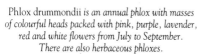

Vegetables

If not completed, dig vegetable plots, incorporating well-decomposed farmyard manure or garden compost. Remove and burn perennial weeds.

Greenhouses

Pack chrysanthemum stools in boxes of loam-based potting compost, water them and place in gentle warmth in a greenhouse.

Phlox drummondii is an annual phlox with masses of colourful heads packed with pink, purple, lavender, red and white flowers from July to September. There are also herbaceous phloxes.

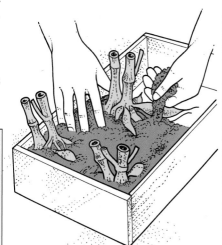

Greenhouses

Put dahlia tubers into boxes, packing loam-based potting compost around their roots. Water and place them in gentle warmth in a greenhouse.

Flowers to sow this month in gentle warmth to produce plants for greenhouse and home decoration

❀ African Violet
   (*Saintpaulia ionantha*)

❀ Cape Primrose
   (*Streptocarpus hybridus*)

❀ Gloxinia
   (*Sinningia speciosa*)

Flowers grown as half-hardy annuals to sow this month in gentle warmth in a greenhouse

❀ African Daisy
   (*Arctosis x hybrida*)

❀ African Marigolds
   (*Tagetes erecta*)

❀ Ageratum
   (*Ageratum houstonianum*)

❀ Alyssum
   (*Alyssum maritimum/Lobularia maritima*)

❀ Annual Phlox
   (*Phlox drummondii*)

❀ Balsam
   (*Impatiens balsamina*)

❀ Bells of Ireland
   (*Molucella laevis*)

❀ Blanket Flower
   (*Gaillardia pulchella*)

February

8

Don't be frugal with half-hardy annuals - to create a stunningly attractive display in flower borders as well as in containers on a patio they must be planted densely. Therefore, raise plenty of plants by sowing seeds this month or during March.

9

10

11

The thornless climber 'Zephirine Drouhin' is ideal for planting close to a doorway or path.

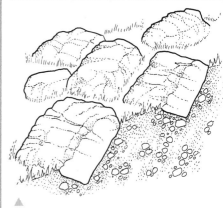

12

13

▲

Create new rock gardens in sunny positions, not under trees. Shade, and leaves falling on plants in autumn, are detrimental, soon causing them to deteriorate. Also, ensure the area is well drained. The stones must slightly tilt backwards. If you do not have space for a rock garden, build a dry-stone wall. It is surprising how many plants can be set in it.

Flowers

If herbaceous plants have not yet been tidied up and old shoots cut down, do this now. Also, lightly fork between plants, spreading well-rotted manure or compost between them.

14

◀ Winter-flowering pansies need a bright, sunny position to encourage a wealth of flowers.

Rock gardens create homes for alpines, bulbs, dwarf conifers and small herbaceous plants. Do not position rock gardens under trees.

Flowers grown as half-hardy annuals to sow this month in gentle warmth in a greenhouse

- Canary Flower
  (*Tropaeolum perigrinum*)
- East Lothian Stocks
  (*Matthiola incana*)
- French Marigold
  (*Tagetes patula*)
- Heliotrope
  (*Heliotropium x hybridum*)
- Kingfisher Daisy
  (*Felicia bergeriana*)
- Livingstone Daisy
  (*Mesembryanthemum criniflorum*)
- Lobelia
  (*Lobelia erinus*)
- Nemesia
  (*Nemesia strumosa*)

Lawns

Where daffodils are naturalized in lawns, cordon off the area to protect the emerging shoots.

Vegetables

When starting a new vegetable garden, first dig the site and remove and burn all perennial weeds. Then, plant a crop of potatoes, setting the tubers 15cm/6in deep, 60cm/2ft apart and in rows with 60-75cm/2-2½ ft between them. Prepare the soil now and plant the potatoes in spring. Using potatoes in this way helps to clear the land of weeds and to break up the soil.

Vegetables

Create a summer screen - as well as an edible one - by sowing a double line of runner bean seeds. Seeds cannot be sown until all risk of frost has passed, but now is the time to prepare the soil. Dig out a trench 30-38cm/12-15in deep and fill its base with well-decayed farmyard manure or garden compost. This helps to retain moisture around the roots. Moisture and sunshine are essential.

Fruit

If you want a plum tree but have space for only one tree, select 'Victoria'. It is self-fertile and good for both cooking and eating.

Plums can be grown against a wall, where they benefit from the warmth and shelter.

Trachycarpus fortunei can be grown outdoors.

Palms to sow this month in warmth for home and conservatory decoration

- Areca Palm
  (*Chrysalidocarpus lutescens*)
- Californian Fan Palm
  (*Washingtonia filifera*)
- Canary Island Palm
  (*Phoenix canariensis*)
- Date Palm
  (*Phoenix dactilifera*)
- European Fan Palm
  (*Chamaerops humilis*)
- Fan Palm
  (*Trachycarpus fortunei*)

Fruit

A shortage of lime in the soil when growing plums, cherries and peaches causes poor stone development. Therefore, before planting these fruits, ensure the soil is slightly alkaline. An inexpensive soil-testing kit will indicate its alkalinity or acidity.

Greenhouses

When buying a greenhouse, work out the size you need, then double it. You will always need more space than initially anticipated.

February

15

16

February fill dyke.

17

Keep lawns short throughout the year to minimize the risk of children becoming infected with *Toxicara*, a parasite transmitted by dogs and cats.

18

19

Rose bushes affected by black spot last year should be tidied up by removing and burning all leaves from around them.

20

Continue to sow tomato seeds to raise plants for growing in greenhouses.

21

Flowers

Prune Winter-flowering Jasmine (Jasminum nudiflorum) as soon as its flowers fade. Cut back flowered shoots to 5-7.5cm/2-3in of their bases. Completely cut out old and weak wood.

Flowers

Romantic, scent-enriched bowers should be planned now. Many roses, as well as several clematis, are scented and will create leafy and floriferous overhead canopies. Use scented annuals to produce scent around its base. Either construct a rustic arch against a wall, or form an arbour with brick pillars and wooden cross beams.

Flowers

Trim winter-flowering heathers as soon as their flowers fade. Use hedge shears to clip lightly over them, creating a gently undulating surface.

Fruit

Inspect fruits in store, removing those that show signs of decay. If left, they cause other fruits to deteriorate.

Flowers to sow this month in gentle warmth to produce plants for greenhouse and home decoration

- ❀ Persian Violet
  (*Exacum affine*)

- ❀ Poison Primrose
  (*Primula obconica*)

- ❀ Temple Bells
  (*Smithiantha hybrida*)

Flowers grown as half-hardy annuals to sow this month in gentle warmth in a greenhouse

- ❀ Marigold
  (*Tagetes tenuifolia/T. signata*)

- ❀ Mask Flower
  (*Alonsoa warscewiczii*)

- ❀ Petunia
  (*Petunia x hybrida*)

- ❀ Prince of Wales' Feather
  (*Celosia argentea plumosa*)

- ❀ Queen Anne's Lace
  (*Didiscus caeruleus/Trachymene caeruleus*)

- ❀ Salvia
  (*Salvia splendens*)

- ❀ Silver Lace
  (*Chrysanthemum ptarmicaeflorum*)

Vegetables ▲

Place cloches along rows where vegetable seeds are to be sown later in the year. This ensures that the soil will be warm and germination rapid. Use glass or plastic to close the ends of the cloches to avoid creating a cold, draughty tunnel.

Primula obconica *flowers from December to May in greenhouses as well as indoors.*

Fruit ▲

Spray peach trees and nectarines against peach leaf curl, a disease that causes leaves to thicken, first becoming greenish-yellow then deep-crimson.

February

22

23

For a fast-growing hedge, plant Leyland Cypress (*Cupressocyparis leylandii*), but remember that when established it grows several feet a year and eventually reaches over 15m/50ft high and 4.5m/15ft wide. It is best as a windbreak and planted at least 30m/100ft from a house.

24

25

Before using a hose or sprinkler to water gardens in summer, ensure that you have a licence and there is not a hosepipe ban in your area

26

27

28/29

Pot up cuttings of perpetual-flowering carnations. Do not give them high temperatures.

Flowers

In warm areas, prune shrubs that flowered late during the previous summer. Pruning now encourages the development of shoots that will bear flowers later in the year.

Flowers

Clean out water-butts, especially if leaves have fallen in them. Tip the barrel over and scrub the inside. Warm water, disinfectant and a scrubbing brush usually removes algae and slime. Afterwards, thoroughly rinse with water.

Vegetables

If, after clearing your garden shed, you have amassed chemicals which you don't want, do not tip them down a drain as they may contaminate water courses. Instead, consult your local authority.

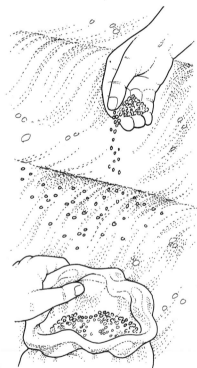

Vegetables

Feed establshed asparagus beds with a general fertilizer at 135gram/sq metre or 4oz/sq yd.

Fruit ▲
Prune autumn-fruiting raspberries now. Cut the canes to within a few inches of the ground.

Fruit
When inserting wooden posts to support fences or fruit canes, first place their bases in deep plastic bags that rise about 15cm/6in above the soil. Tie each bag's top closely to its stake. And ensure that a 'cap' is nailed to the top of the post to prevent water entering the wood.

Greenhouses
Pot up the tuber-like, scaly rhizomes of achimines, five or six to a 13cm/5in pot, using a loam-based potting compost. Set the rhizomes about 2.5cm/1in deep, water and place the pots in 16°C/61°F. Increase the amount of water as shoots develop.

Palms to sow this month in warmth for home and conservatory decoration

❀ Kentia Palm
  (*Howeia forsteriana*)

❀ Mexican Fan Palm
  (*Washingtonia robusta*)

❀ Parlour Palm
  (*Chamaedorea elegans*)

❀ Pygmy Date Palm
  (*Phoenix roebelenii*)

Flowers grown as half-hardy annuals to sow this month in gentle warmth in a greenhouse

❀ Snapdragon
  (*Antirrhinum majus*)

❀ Slipper Flower
  (*Calceolaria integrifolia/C. rugosa*)

❀ Spider Flower
  (*Cleome spinosa*)

❀ Tassel Flower
  (*Emilia flammea*)

❀ Tobacco Plant
  (*Nicotiana alata/N. affinis*)

❀ Verbena
  (*Verbena x hybrida*)

❀ Wax Plant
  (*Begonia semperflorens*)

Begonia semperflorens, the Wax Plant, is superb in summer-bedding displays. It can also be planted in window-boxes, troughs and around the edges of tubs on patios.

Nicotiana is known for its intense evening scent.

March

The winds of March blow hard and cold
But the gardener has nought to fear
A well-kept garden stands proud and bold
All ready for the coming year

March

1

*For every fog in March,
There'll be a frost in May.*

2

Sow sweet pea seeds 12mm/½in deep in
seedtrays and place in 61-68°C/16-20°F.
They can also be sown outdoors in April
in the garden.

*Sweet Peas are some of the loveliest
flowers for decorating rooms in summer.*

3

Sow celery seeds in boxes or pots in
greenhouses, placing them in
13-16°C/55-61°F.

4

5

6

7

When buying houseplants, avoid those
with roots coming out of drainage holes in
their pots. Also, do not buy plants with
pots covered with moss or algae, flowers
fully open, or stems bare of leaves.
Additionally, discard large plants in small
pots or small plants in large pots.

Flowers

Plant container-grown shrubs at any
time when the soil is not frozen or
waterlogged. Prepare the planting site,
forking-in a light dressing of bonemeal.
Dig out a hole large enough to
accommodate the container, and form a
small mound of soil in its base. Water
the plant a few hours being setting it in
the soil. Remove the container and
spread out the roots, with the top of the
soil-ball slightly lower than the
surrounding soil. It may be necessary to
adjust the height of the mound. Firm soil
around the roots.

- ❀ African Violet
  (*Saintpaulia ionantha*)

- ❀ Cape Primrose
  (*Streptocarpus hybridus*)

- ❀ Poison Primrose
  (*Primula obconica*)

- ❀ Flaming Katy
  (*Kalanchoe blossfeldiana*)

Pink-mauve ageratums complement deep-violet petunias.

Flowers

Do not leave foliage houseplants continually in one position, as leaves and stems grow towards the light and eventually create an unsightly plant. Instead, turn the plant a quarter of a turn every few days.

Lawns

Grass cutting begins soon. For the first cut, set the blades high, gradually reducing their height as the season progresses.

Below left: When planting container-grown shrubs, take care when removing the container not to damage the plant's roots.
Below: After putting the plant in the hole and covering with soil, gently use your foot to firm soil around the roots.

Vegetables

From now and until May, sow radishes thinly in drills 12mm/½in deep and 25cm/10in apart.

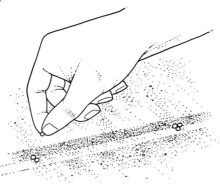

Vegetables

Sow parsnip seeds in groups of three, 15-20cm/6-8in part, 12mm/½in deep and in drills 38cm/15in apart. These are later thinned to the strongest seedling at each position.

Greenhouses

Take chrysanthemum cuttings, 6.5-7.5cm/2-½-3in long. Remove the lower leaves, trim beneath a leaf-joint and insert 18-25mm/¾-1in deep in equal parts moist peat and sharp sand. Water and place in gentle warmth.

- ❀ African Daisy
  (*Arctosis x hybrida*)

- ❀ African Marigolds
  (*Tagetes erecta*)

- ❀ Ageratum
  (*Ageratum houstonianum*)

- ❀ Alyssum
  (*Alyssum maritimum/Lobularia maritima*)

- ❀ Annual Phlox
  (*Phlox drummondii*)

- ❀ Bachelor's Buttons
  (*Gomphrena globosa*)

- ❀ Balsam
  (*Impatiens balsamina*)

- ❀ Barberton Daisy
  (*Gerbera jamesonii*)

- ❀ Bells of Ireland
  (*Molucella laevis*)

- ❀ Blanket Flower
  (*Gaillardia pulchella*)

March

8

9

March winds and April showers,
Bring forth May flowers.

10

11

Sow onion seeds thinly in drills 12mm
/½in deep and 23-30cm/9-12in apart.

12

13

14

◄ Giving houseplants the exact amount of
water they need is difficult, but using
moisture-indicator strips helps to make
this job easier.

Flowers ▲

Lift and divide large, congested clumps
of herbaceous plants. Use a garden fork
to dig under the clump and to prise it
gently apart. Replant young parts from
around the outside. Discard the old,
woody, central parts.

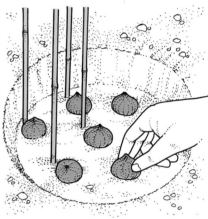

Flowers ▲

Plant gladioli (13-15cm/5-6in deep) in
small groups, each corm about 20cm/8in
apart. Before covering, insert stakes by
the side of each corm.

Flowers

Plant *Ranunculus asiaticus* tubers
(5cm/2in deep) and lily bulbs (usually
about two-and-a-half times their depth)
if the soil is workable. However, the
Madonna Lily (*Lilium candidum*) is
planted with its nose just below the
surface.

Lawns

Repair edges, especially where soil has fallen against the lawn.

Vegetables

Sow broad beans 7.5cm/3in deep and 20cm/8in apart in drills 25-30cm/10-12in apart. Usually, they are sown in double rows, with a 60cm/2ft wide path between each pair.

Fruit

Soft fruits can still be planted. Also, check plants put in earlier, re-firming soil loosened by frost.

Greenhouses

Take cuttings of pelargoniums. Trim off the lower leaves, cutting stems below leaf-joints and inserting them into sandy compost. Place in gentle warmth.

Greenhouse

Take cuttings of dahlias, fuchsias and perpetual-flowering carnations.

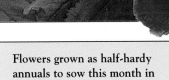

The trumpet-shaped Lilium candidum is one of the most spectacular lilies for garden display.

Flowers grown as half-hardy annuals to sow this month in gentle warmth in a greenhouse

❀ Canary Flower
(*Tropaeolum peregrinum*)

❀ China Aster
(*Callistephus chinensis*)

❀ East Lothian Stocks
(*Matthiola incana*)

❀ French Marigold
(*Tagetes patula*)

❀ Heliotrope
(*Heliotropium x hybridum*)

❀ Kingfisher Daisy
(*Felicia bergeriana*)

❀ Livingstone Daisy
(*Mesembryanthemum criniflorum*)

❀ Lobelia
(*Lobelia erinus*)

❀ Nemesia
(*Nemesia strumosa*)

Above: A beautiful variety of pelargonium, aptly named 'Jewel'.

Below: The exquisite fuchsia 'Perky Pink', an undeniably beautiful plant.

Organic Gardening

Gardens that attract butterflies are popular. In spring, *Alyssum saxatile*, Aubrietia and Forget-me-nots are appealing to them.

March

15

16

Sow carrots thinly in drills 12-18mm/
½-¾in deep and 23cm/9in apart.

17

18

Sow early peas, 10cm/4in apart in drills
5cm/2in deep.

19

20

21

Dahlia 'Shoesmith Salmon'

Flowers
In mild areas, plant dahlia tubers that
have been stored during winter but have
not developed shoots. Cover the tubers
with 7.5cm/3in of soil.

Flowers
Remove glass tents and cloches earlier
put over alpine plants to prevent rain
damaging them. Wear gloves and place
the glass where it will not be a danger to
animals or children.

Lawns
Brush and scatter worm casts. If left and
trodden on they create muddy patches
and kill grass seedlings.

Vegetables
Plant young cauliflowers raised from
seeds sown in a greenhouse in January.
Plant them 60cm/2ft apart in rows
60cm/2ft apart. Ensure the soil is well
firmed around their roots.

◀ If a houseplant wilts because the compost
is dry, revive it by standing the pot in a
bowl of water. Also, mist-spray plants
with smooth-surfaced leaves.

Fruit

Place cloches over a few strawberry plants to encourage early fruiting. It also prevents rain damaging the fruits.

Greenhouses

Pot up cyclamen seedlings. The corms must be at compost level - if excessively deep they will not develop properly, but if too high they become dry and hard.

Greenhouses

Plant Gloxinia (*Sinningia*) tubers, setting them slightly apart and packing moist peat around them. Water and place them in gentle warmth. When shoots appear, pot them into small pots.

Flowers to sow this month in gentle warmth to produce plants for greenhouse and home decoration

* Gloxinia
  (*Sinningia speciosa*)

* Persian Violet
  (*Exacum affine*)

* Temple Bells
  (*Smithiantha hybrida*)

Celosia argentea plumosa *creates fluffy spires in pink, yellow, crimson and amber.*

Flowers grown as half-hardy annuals to sow this month in gentle warmth in a greenhouse

* Marigold
  (*Tagetes tenuifolia/T. signata*)

* Mask Flower
  (*Alonsoa warscewiczii*)

* Matricaria
  (*Chrysanthemum parthenium*)

* Petunia
  (*Petunia x hybrida*)

* Prince of Wales' Feather
  (*Celosia argentea plumosa*)

* Prince's Feather
  (*Amaranthus hypochondriacus*)

* Queen Anne's Lace
  (*Didiscus caeruleus*)

* Salvia
  (*Salvia splendens*)

* Silver Lace
  (*Chrysanthemum ptarmicaeflorum*)

French Marigold 'Queen Sophia' *grows in full sun*

March

22

23

Continue to take cuttings of dahlias.

24

25

Remove dead flower heads from bulbs that
have flowered. If left, they produce seeds
at the expense of bulb development.

26

27

28

Pot on all plants that fill their pots
with roots.

*Above: A pond often forms a centrepiece in a
garden and seldom fails to capture attention. Do
not position it under trees.*

Flowers
Garden ponds are eye-catching features.
They are usually created from either a
rigid glassfibre shell, which is set in a
hole dug to fit it, or a flexible plastic
liner. The quality and thickness of the
liner determines its life span.

Flowers ▶
Small baskets planted with pansies,
polyanthas, small-leaved and variegated
ivies, heathers and cyclamineus-type
narcissi create displays ideal for sheltered
patios and cold porches. Keep the
compost moist, but not continually
saturated.

Flowers
Plant bare-rooted rose bushes. Unpack the plants and stand them in water. Trim off damaged roots and cut back long shoots to outward-pointing buds. Position them in the ground so that the old soil-mark on the stem is fractionally below the surface. This allows for soil settlement. Firm soil around the roots.

Vegetables
In mild areas, plant early potatoes, 15cm/6in deep and 30cm/12in apart in rows 60cm/2ft apart. In cold areas, delay planting for three or four weeks.

Vegetables
Plant onion sets 10-15cm/4-6in apart in rows 30cm/12in apart. The necks of the sets must be just above the soil's surface.

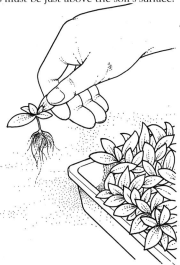

Flowers grown as half-hardy annuals to sow this month in gentle warmth in a greenhouse

- ❀ Snapdragon
  (*Antirrhinum majus*)

- ❀ Slipper Flower
  (*Calceolaria integrifolia/C. rugosa*)

- ❀ Spider Flower
  (*Cleome spinosa*)

- ❀ Summer Cypress
  (*Kochia scoparia 'Trichophylla'*)

- ❀ Tassel Flower
  (*Emilia flammea*)

- ❀ Tobacco Plant
  (*Nicotiana alata/N. affinis*)

- ❀ Verbena
  (*Verbena x hybrida*)

- ❀ Wax Plant
  (*Begonia semperflorens*)

- ❀ Zinnia
  (*Zinnia elegans*)

Greenhouses
Prick out young seedlings before they become congested. Hold each seedling by one of its leaves, not its stem. And do not allow their roots to become dry.

Greenhouses
Increase the amount of ventilation but avoid creating draughts. Open the ventilators on the leeside. Automatic ventilators help to make this job easier.

Greenhouses
Increase the amount of water given to plants in pots in greenhouses and indoors. But ensure the compost is not continually saturated as this kills roots. If the compost does become waterlogged, remove the pot and wrap kitchen towel around the soil-ball. When dry, repot into a clean pot.

March

29

March comes in like a lion, goes out like a lamb.

31

30

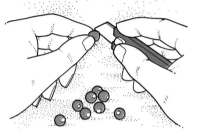

When sowing large seeds with hard coats, such as sweet peas, either nick the seed's coat with a sharp knife or scrape with a nail-file. This allows the seed readily to absorb moisture, an essential stage in germination.

The sweetly scented Rose 'Fragrant Delight'.

Flowers ▲

When pruning roses, always cut fractionally above an outward-pointing bud. If long snags are left, this encourages the onset of decay, while if too close there is the risk of the bud being damaged.

Flowers

Prune Hybrid Tea (Large-flowered Roses) and Floribunda (Cluster-flowered Roses) now.

Apple trees following the line of a curved garden wall. Trees trained in this way should have their blossom protected from severe frosts.

Convolvulus tricolor *can be sown outdoors this month, where it is to flower. Any well-drained garden soil will do. Choose a sunny situation.*

Lawns

Use a lawn roller to level turf slightly lifted by frost. However, do not expect a roller to level large mounds. Remember that rolling consolidates soil and restricts aeration.

Vegetables

Prick out celery seedlings sown earlier in the year in a greenhouse. Space them 5cm/2in apart. Leave the seedbox in gentle warmth in a greenhouse for a week, then place in a garden frame, slowly hardening off the plants.

Fruit

Protect blossom on wall-trained fruit trees if frost is expected. Either hook up or tie dry hessian or sacks over the flowers or, if low, place a garden frame over them.

Greenhouses

Harden off sweet peas sown earlier in the year in a greenhouse. Reduce temperature, then put them in a garden frame.

Hardy annuals to sow outdoors this month, where they are to flower

❀ Annual Chrysanthemum
(*Chrysanthemum carinatum/C. tricolor*)

❀ Annual Woodruff
(*Asperula azurea/A. setosa*)

❀ Californian Poppy
(*Eschscholzia californica*)

❀ Clarkia
(*Clarkia elegans*)

❀ Clarkia
(*Clarkia pulchella*)

❀ Convolvulus
(*Convolvulus tricolor/C.minor*)

❀ Cornflower
(*Centaurea cyanus*)

❀ Larkspur
(*Delphinium ajacis*)

❀ Love-lies-Bleeding
(*Amaranthus caudatus*)

❀ Pheasant's Eye
(*Adonis aestivalis*)

❀ Pot Marigold
(*Calendula officinalis*)

❀ Star of the Veldt
(*Dimorphotheca aurantiaca*)

❀ Swan River Daisy
(*Brachycome iberidifolia*)

❀ Viper's Bugloss
(*Echium lycopsis*)

April

Spring-like sunshine arrives at last
As April days now warm the earth
Cruel winter is but a memory past-
Once again the world gives birth

April

1

2

A red sky in the morning,
Is a shepherd's warning,
A red sky at night,
Is a shepherd's delight.

3

4

April showers bring forth May flowers.

5

6

Plant greenhouse tomato plants in the border soil, growing-bags or pots.

7

Patio tubs packed with bright-faced polyanthus - perhaps encircling a yellow-foliaged, cone-shaped dwarf conifer - bring a burst of spring colour to patios. These plants can be set in a tub now.

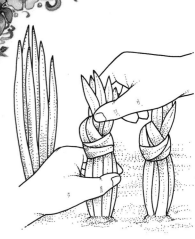

Flowers ▲
As early daffodils fade, remove the flower heads but leave their leaves intact. Allow them to die down naturally. To keep them tidy, bend their leaves over and secure with elastic-bands or twine. Alternatively, tie in knots.

Lawns
Prepare sites in readiness for sowing seeds. If the area is wet and sticky, leave this job until the end of the month. Dig the site - if not previously undertaken in winter - and break up the soil. Rake level, removing stones of more than 2.5cm/1in in size. Leave smaller ones, as they assist in drainage. Ensure all perennial weeds have been removed. Check that the site is level - or evenly sloped - by knocking pegs into the ground and placing a spirit-level across them.

Vegetables
Prepare a seedbed by digging the soil, then lightly consolidating and levelling it. Then sow Brussels sprouts seeds. Later, transplant them to their growing positions.

Fruit trees
Prune plums and gages as soon as their sap starts to rise. If pruned in winter, when dormant, there is a risk of diseases entering cuts.

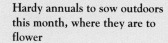

Fruit trees

Spray fruit trees and bushes with pesticides and insecticides before bud-burst or after petal-fall. This helps to reduce the number of pollinating insects killed by chemical sprays.

Greenhouses ▲

If congested with seedlings and newly-sown seedboxes, make further space in greenhouses by the addition of temporary shelves suspended from wires attached to the glazing bars. But take care, as they may easily be tipped over. Additionally, ensure that when watering plants on these shelves moisture does not drip on those below. Special shelving can be bought for fixing to aluminium greenhouses.

Lavatera trimestris is an annual mallow.

Flowers to sow this month in gentle warmth to produce plants for greenhouse and home decoration

❈ Temple Bells
  (*Smithiantha hybrida*)

❈ Cineraria
  (*Senecio cruentus*)

❈ Poison Primula
  (*Primula obconica*)

❈ Flaming Katy
  (*Kalanchoe blossfeldiana*)

❈ Persian Violet
  (*Exacum affine*)

Hardy annuals to sow outdoors this month, where they are to flower

❈ Annual Chrysanthemum
  (*Chrysanthemum carinatum*)

❈ Annual Mallow
  (*Lavatera trimestris*)

❈ Annual Woodruff
  (*Asperula orientalis*)

❈ Baby Blue Eyes
  (*Nemophila menziesii*)

❈ Californian Poppy
  (*Eschscholzia californica*)

❈ Chalk Flower
  (*Gypsophila elegans*)

Above: Gypsophila elegans is peppered with flowers.

Left: Cinerarias are ideal houseplants.

Organic Gardening

Ladybird larvae and adults eat greenfly (aphids). Lacewings and hoverflies also kill this major pest. Therefore, encourage these natural predators by not indiscriminately spraying them with insecticides.

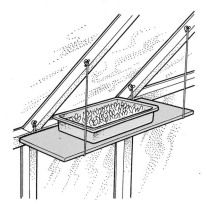

April

8

9

Rain before seven,
Fine before eleven.

10

11

It is not spring until you can plant your foot
upon twelve daisies.

12

13

There's rosemary, that's for remembrance;
pray, love, remember:
and there is pansies,
that's for thoughts.
William Shakespeare - Hamlet

14

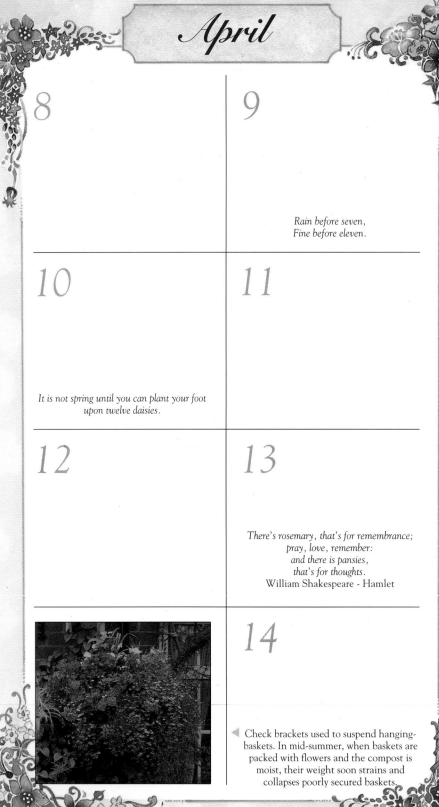

◀ Check brackets used to suspend hanging-
baskets. In mid-summer, when baskets are
packed with flowers and the compost is
moist, their weight soon strains and
collapses poorly secured baskets.

Flowers

Prune winter-flowering shrubs now, and
spring-flowering types as soon as their
flowers fade. Winter-flowering shrubs
require little pruning, other than the
removal of dead or damaged shoots, as
well as tidying up the plant's shape.

Spring-flowering shrubs, however,
need more extensive pruning. Because
their flowers are borne mainly on shoots
which developed during the middle or
late part of the previous season, cut out a
few of the oldest shoots from the base.
This encourages the development of
fresh shoots that will bear flowers during
the following spring. Also, remove dead
wood and twiggy growths from the
plant's centre.

Lawns

Soil preparation for seed sowing can be
completed now. To consolidate the soil
evenly, systematically tread over it,
shuffling sideways across the plot and
each time firming a strip about
25cm/10in wide. Rake the surface level
and add a general fertilizer, mixing it
into the top 2.5cm/1in. The same
thorough soil preparation is needed for
sowing seeds and when laying turf.

Organic Gardening

Don't throw away kitchen waste, lawn-mowings and other soft material from plants. Place it on a compost heap, where it will decompose and later be either dug into the soil or used to form a 5-7.5cm/2-3in thick mulch around plants. This conserves moisture in the soil, prevents the growth of weeds and provides plant foods.

Left: Colourful poppies which, despite their delicate appearance, do not need staking. It is necessary, however, to remove dead flowers to prevent them scattering seeds.

Hardy annuals to sow outdoors this month, where they are to flower

❀ Clarkia
(Clarkia elegans)

❀ Field Poppy
(Papaver rhoeas)

❀ Flower-of-an-Hour
(Hibiscus trionum)

❀ Godetia
(Godetia grandiflora)

❀ Larkspur
(Delphinium ajacis)

❀ Love-in-a-Mist
(Nigella damascena)

Below: Stately delphiniums, whose long-lasting flowers are ideal for flower arrangements.

Vegetables ▲
Sow seeds of cabbages for harvesting during summer and autumn. Sow seeds 18mm/¾in deep in drills 15cm/6in apart in a seedbed. The young plants are later planted in a vegetable garden.

Vegetables
Sow parsley seed in pots, then place in 10-15°C/50-59°F.

Greenhouses
Cyclamen plants that have finished flowering need drying. Place the pots on their sides under the greenhouse staging, in a dry place.

April

15

Clear moon, frost soon

16

17

18

Prepare new asparagus beds - dig trenches 38cm/15in wide and 30cm/12in deep.

19

Who'll buy my sweet blooming lavender? Sixteen full branches for a penny.

20

21

◀ Check trellises and wires supporting climbers before these plants develop leaves and clothe their supports. Winter winds, frost and snow often dislodge supports. Re-drill holes and use new fixings and screws.

Flowers

Harden off summer bedding plants sown earlier in the year in a greenhouse or conservatory. They must be slowly accustomed to outside conditions - do not expose them to frost.

Lawns

Sow lawn seed about a week after the soil has been levelled, firmed and fertilizers added. Sow seeds evenly at 35-70 grams/sq. metre (1-2oz/sq. yd). Stretch strings across the area to form metre- or yard-wide squares and in each area evenly scatter seed. Then, lightly rake it in to the surface soil. Select a seed mixture suitable for the site's shadiness and likely wear. Mixtures with finely-bladed grasses should be reserved for ornamental areas, where wear is restricted.

Vegetables

Sow salad onions 12mm/½in deep in drills 13-15cm/5-6in apart.

Vegetables

Sow garden peas 10cm/4in apart in drills 5cm/2in deep, and summer spinach 18-25mm/½-1in deep in drills 30cm/12in apart.

Nasturtiums grow well in poor, sandy soils.

Greenhouses ▲

Tomatoes sown earlier in the year and planted in a greenhouse will now be producing sideshoots. Remove these by bending and snapping them sideways.

Greenhouses ▲

Sow melons and cucumbers for growing in a greenhouse. Sow two seeds 12mm/½in deep in each pot, thinning them later to the strongest seedling. Place in 18°C/64°F.

Hardy annuals to sow outdoors this month, where they are to flower

❀ Love-lies-bleeding
   (*Amaranthus caudatus*)

❀ Mignonette
   (*Reseda odorata*)

❀ Nasturtium
   (*Tropaeolum majus*)

❀ Night-scented Stock
   (*Matthiola bicornis*)

❀ Pheasant's Eye
   (*Adonis aestivalis*)

Organic Gardening

Recycle broken wire coat-hangers. Bend them to form a framework that can be covered with polythene bags. They are ideal for covering early plants, protecting them from frost and cold winds.

Night-scented Stocks are a popular feature in cottage gardens, growing happily in full sun or light shade.

April

22

23

Rain, rain, go away,
Come again another day.

24

25

Rain on Good Friday or Easter Day,
A good crop of grass but a bad one of hay.

26

27

When pricking out seedlings, hold them
by their leaves - not their stems.

28

Order hanging-baskets from patio-plant
specialists to avoid disappointment
later.

Flowers ▲

Plant waterlilies and other water plants.
Select the variety of waterlily to suit the
depth of the pond. Put them in plastic-
mesh containers that initially can be
stood on bricks to ensure they are at the
right height - leaves level with the
water's surface. As plants grow, the
bricks can be removed.

Waterlilies grow well in open, sunny positions.

Hardy annuals to sow outdoors this month where they are to flower

- ❀ Poached Egg Plant
  (*Limnanthes douglasii*)

- ❀ Pot Marigold
  (*Calendula officinalis*)

- ❀ Scarlet Flax
  (*Linum grandiflorum*)

- ❀ Snow on the Mountain
  (*Euphorbia marginata*)

- ❀ Stardust
  (*Gilia lutea*)

Left: The Scarlet Flax creates a mass of saucer-shaped flowers from June to August. It is essential to sow it in full sun.

Below: A well-kept vegetable garden is a pleasure to work in. Rotating crops helps to control pests and diseases, and keeps the soil in good condition.

Lawns

Lawn seed germinates within seven to ten days of being sown. If the weather is hot and dry during this period, thoroughly but lightly water the soil so that the top few inches are moist. Just dampening the surface will do more harm than good. Covering the area with clear polythene - immediately after seeds have been sown - keeps the soil moist and warm. Keep the polythene in place with bricks or pieces of wood. Remove it when the grass seedlings are about 2.5cm/1in high.

Vegetables

Sow radishes 12mm/½in deep in rows 20-30cm/8-12in apart.

Vegetables

Sow maincrop potatoes 15cm/6in deep and 38cm/15in apart in rows 75cm/2-½ft apart. This ensures that there is plenty of room for their development.

Organic Gardening

Plan vegetable gardens so that similar types of plants are not grown on the same plot every year. Rotate crops: first potatoes; then root crops (carrots, turnips and parsnips); the following year brassicas (cabbages and Brussels Sprouts); and, lastly, legumes (peas and beans). Rotating crops helps to prevent the build up of pests and diseases, as well as keeping the soil in good condition.

Greenhouses

Continue to remove sideshoots from tomato plants. Also, harden off summer-flowering plants in readiness for planting into the garden when all risk of frost has passed.

April

29

*Mackerel sky,
Not long dry.*

30

Always sow seeds thinly. Congested seedlings become weak and spindly and encourage the presence of diseases.

Above: Few sights are more impressive in a garden than a beautifully kept lawn.

Attractive and novel containers for a spring or summer display on a patio can be created from three or four car tyres. Scrub the tyres, stack them on top of each other and wire each one to its neighbour. Place several bricks inside, so that a large plastic bucket - with holes in its base - can be stood on them, with its rim level with the top of the tyres. Paint the tyres with matt-white emulsion paint. Place drainage material in the bucket's base, fill with potting compost and pack with patio-brightening plants.

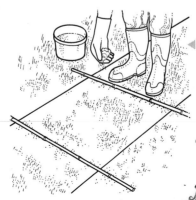

A successful herbaceous border creates colour and texture throughout summer.

Flowers
Keep herbaceous borders free from weeds, taking care not to damage young shoots that may be developing from established plants. When shoots are about 10cm/4in high, insert twiggy shoots around each clump so that stems grow up and through them. This gives support without being obtrusive.

Lawns
Feed established lawns with a quick-acting lawn fertilizer at 70 grams/sq metre (2oz/sq yd). Use string and canes to mark the lawn into metre or yard squares.

Fruit
Prune peaches and nectarines as soon as buds start to develop. Do not prune 'stone' fruits in winter, when they are dormant.

Above: Sunflowers may reach 3m/10ft or more in height; but there are many smaller varieties.

Greenhouse
Increasingly, open the ventilators on greenhouses to prevent the temperature rising too high. Avoid draughts on plants.

Greenhouses ▲
Spring is the time when pests and diseases start to devastate plants. Check all plants thoroughly, especially under their leaves, in joints between leaf-stalks and stems, around soft shoot tips and flower buds.

Hardy annuals to sow outdoors this month, where they are to flower

❀ Sunflower
  (*Helianthus annuus*)

❀ Sweet Sultan
  (*Centaurea moschata*)

❀ Toadflax
  (*Linaria maroccana*)

❀ Virginian Stock
  (*Malcolmia maritima*)

Organic Gardening ▲
Put small collars of felt around young cabbage plants to prevent cabbage root flies going down stems to attack the roots.

May

Lilac and cherry bloom in May
And soon the trees are clothed in leaves
Before the month has passed halfway
Winter's blast is summer's breeze

May

1

2

A swarm of bees in May is worth a load of hay.

3

4

Remove runners from strawberry plants to direct their energies into fruit production.

5

6

7 1997 Transplanted pelina Aubrelia B12 L.2

Soil at the bases of walls soon becomes dry. Therefore, before planting climbers and wall shrubs in these areas, ensure that the soil is moist and contains plenty of organic material, such as well-decomposed compost, that will retain moisture. It will also be necessary to water these plants regularly until their roots are established.

When filling ponds, tie a piece of cloth over the end of the hosepipe to prevent jets of water disturbing plants and soil. Alternatively, stand a bucket on bricks in the centre of the pond, secure the end of a hosepipe to it and run water so that it trickles out of the bucket and into the pond.

Flowers
Thin hardy annuals sown earlier, initially to 10cm/4in apart, later to twice that spacing. Re-firm soil around each seedling.If left loose, roots are not in close contact with soil and will become dry.

Vegetables
Sow asparagus peas 10cm/4in apart in drills 2.5cm/1in deep and 38-45cm/15-18in apart. When plants are a few inches high, support them with twiggy sticks.

Vegetables
Sow runner bean seeds outside in areas where the risk of frost after the third week in May is remote. If poles are to be used to support plants, put these in first. If supported by strings, these can be put up later. When supported by poles, sow two or three seeds, 5cm/2in deep and 10-15cm/4-6in apart, at the base of each support. If in rows and supported by strings, sow seeds 15cm/6in apart, 5cm/2in deep and in rows 60cm/2ft apart.

Fruit

Mulch established raspberry canes with well-rotted manure or compost to keep the soil moist, cool and nourished. Also, mulch blackcurrant bushes, but first ensure that the soil is moist.

Above: The Fairy Primrose brings colour to greenhouses and homes from December to April.

Below: Aubretia cascades down a wall. This rock garden plant can be invasive if unchecked.

Herbaceous perennials to sow outdoors this month in a seedbed

❀ Anchusa
  (*Anchusa azurea*)

❀ Aubrietia
  (*Aubrietia deltoidea*)

❀ Cupid's Dart
  (*Catananche caerulea*)

❀ Delphinium
  (*Delphinium elatum*)

❀ Globe Thistle
  (*Echinops ritro*)

Flowers to sow this month in gentle warmth for greenhouse and home decoration

❀ Cineraria
  (*Senecio cruentus*)

❀ Dusty Primula
  (*Primula x kewensis*)

❀ Fairy Primrose
  (*Primula malacoides*)

❀ Slipper Flower
  (*Calceolaria x herbeohybrida*)

Hardy annuals to sow outdoors this month where they are to flower

❀ Alyssum
  (*Alyssum maritimum/Lobularia maritima*)

❀ Anchusa
  (*Anchusa capensis*)

❀ Annual Chrysanthemum
  (*Chrysanthemum carinatum*)

❀ Annual Mallow
  (*Lavatera trimestris*)

❀ Annual Woodruff
  (*Asperula orientalis*)

❀ Baby Blue Eyes
  (*Nemophila menziesii*)

❀ Californian Poppy
  (*Eschscholzia californica*)

Organic Gardening

Counteract carrot flies by masking this vegetable's attraction to pests by growing them next to onions. Alternatively, every fortnight scatter lawn-mowings between the rows.

May

8

9

When sowing seeds outdoors, mark the ends of the rows and clearly record the variety and date. Also, label seed pots and boxes.

10

11

Rambler roses will be making long shoots from their bases. Tie these to supports.

12

13

◀ If the weather becomes hot, with strong sunlight, the glass will need shading. Either paint white shading material on the outside or use blinds.

14

Flowers

Remove spring-flowering bedding plants as their flowers fade. Discard plants such as Forget-me-nots and Wallflowers, but carefully fork out bulbs, placing them in shallow trenches in out-of-the way places in the garden. Later, when their leaves have died down, place the bulbs in boxes and store them in a cool, airy, vermin-proof shed until late summer, when they can be replanted.

Lawns

Lawn seed sown in April soon germinates and reaches 7.5cm/3in high, when it can be cut. Use a sharp-bladed mower and cut the grass 5cm/2in high - no shorter. Do not use blunt mowers that tear young seedlings from the soil.

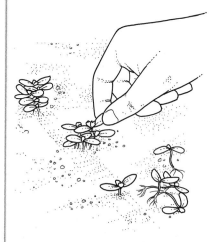

Vegetables ▲

Sow beetroot seeds 18mm/¾in deep in small clusters 13cm/5in apart in rows 30cm/12in apart. Later, thin them to one strong plant at each position.

Vegetables

Sow chicory 12mm/½in deep in drills 38cm/15in apart, and radishes 12mm/½in deep in rows 20-30cm/8-12in apart.

Vegetables

Thin summer lettuces to 23-30cm/9-12in apart.

Above: Aquilegias are short-lived perennials.
Plant them in well-drained soil and light shade.

Herbaceous perennials to outdoor sow this month in a seedbed

- ❀ Granny's Bonnet
  (*Aquilegia vulgaris*)
- ❀ Michaelmas Daisy
  (*Aster novi-belgii*)
- ❀ Midsummer Daisy
  (*Erigeron speciosus*)

Organic Gardening

Deter flea beetles by sowing a thin line of mustard seed around the seedbed where cabbages and other brassica plants are being raised.

Below: Erigeron is a colourful border plant, blooming from June to August.

Hardy annuals to sow outdoors this month where they are to flower

- ❀ Candytuft
  (*Iberis umbellata*)
- ❀ Chalk Flower
  (*Gypsophila elegans*)
- ❀ Cornflower
  (*Centaurea cyanus*)
- ❀ Clarkia
  (*Clarkia elegans*)
- ❀ Convolvulus
  (*Convolvulus tricolor/C. minor*)
- ❀ Cosmea
  (*Cosmos bipinnatus*)
- ❀ Field Poppy
  (*Papaver rhoeas*)

Greenhouse ▲

Regularly clean the leaves of houseplants. Dust and dirt are the enemies of leaves, spoiling their appearance, clogging pores and preventing sunlight reaching them. Wipe large leaves with a damp cloth and dip smaller ones in a bowl of clean water. Do not wet the leaves when plants are in strong sunlight. Use a small, soft brush to remove dirt from hairy-leaved plants and bristly cacti.

May

15

16

Eradicate weeds from between soft fruits by shallow hoeing.

17

18

Watch out for aphids on roses. Spray as necessary.

19

20

21

Indoors and in greenhouses, encourage plantlets at the ends of long stems on Spider Plants (*Chlorophytum comosum*) to root by pegging them into small pots of compost. Secure the plantlets with small, U-shaped pieces of wire. Sever the stems to the parent plant when they have developed roots.

Lawns

Create new lawns from turves. Such lawns can be used within a month of being laid. Thorough soil preparations is essential (see April). Lay turves in rows with their joints staggered. Brush sifted soil between the joints. If the surface is dry, use a light roller to firm them into position. During dry periods, water the entire area.

Lawns

Use selective weedkillers on established lawns when the grass is growing strongly. Do not use weedkillers if the soil is exceptionally dry or wet - and not on young lawns. Afterwards, do not cut the grass for about a week and never put the cuttings on a compost heap. Instead, burn them.

Vegetables

Carefully earth-up potato shoots, using a draw-hoe to pull soil around them - but do not cover their tips.

Vegetables

Mixing seeds with a gel such as wallpaper paste helps them to germinate rapidly in dry conditions. Squeeze the mixture out of a plastic bag and into a drill watered the previous day.

Fruit

If you have fruit in a wire cage or under fine-mesh netting, open up one side to allow pollinating insects to enter.

Greenhouses ▲

Continue to remove sideshoots from tomato plants. If plants are neglected at this stage, they become like a jungle and the crop is diminished.

Herbaceous perennials to sow outdoors this month in a seedbed

* Shasta Daisy
  (*Chrysanthemum maximum*)

* Sneezewort
  (*Achillea ptarmica*)

* Sweet Rocket
  (*Hesperis matronalis*)

* Valerian
  (*Centranthus ruber*)

* Yarrow
  (*Achillea filipendula*)

* Yarrow
  (*Achillea millefolium*)

Left: Hesperis matronalis *is very sweetly scented.*

Below: Achillea *is superb in flower arrangements.*

Hardy annuals to sow outdoors this month where they are to flower

* Flower-of-an-hour
  (*Hibiscus trionum*)

* Larkspur
  (*Delphinium ajacis*)

* Love-in-a-Mist
  (*Nigella damascena*)

* Love-lies-bleeding
  (*Amaranthus caudatus*)

* Mignonette
  (*Reseda odorata*)

* Nasturtium
  (*Tropaeolum majus*)

* Night-scented Stock
  (*Matthiola bicornis*)

Organic Gardening

Don't kill centipedes. Unlike millepedes, which chew plants, centipedes eat insects pests such as grubs, slugs, woodlice and leather jackets. Centipedes have one pair of legs on each body segment, whereas millepedes have two and are slow moving.

May

22

23

Continue to sow peas, carrots, radishes and salad onions.

24

25

If large gooseberry fruits are desired on dessert varieties, thin them slightly.

26

27

28

Keep grass short around fruit trees. If long, it retards the establishment of young trees.

Flowers
Plant summer-flowering bedding plants that have been thoroughly hardened off. In warm areas this job can be tackled earlier, while in extremely cold regions, where frosts may occur until the first week in June, delay planting for a week.

Flowers
Where naturalized bulbs are overcrowded, lift, divide and replant them.

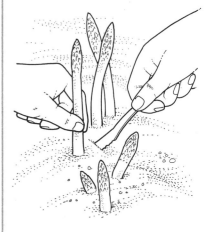

Vegetables ▲
Harvest asparagus spears when 15cm/6in high. Use an asparagus knife to sever them 10cm/4in below the surface.

Myosotis will need watering in dry weather.

Vegetables ▲

Plant leeks when about 15cm/6in long in holes 10-15cm/4-6in deep and 23cm/9in apart in rows 30-38cm/12-15in apart. Trim off long leaves and straggly roots, then drop one plant in each hole. Do not pack the hole with soil, just water each plant.

Greenhouses

Birds and cats invade greenhouses when ventilators and doors are left open. Cover ventilators with netting or wire-mesh. For doors, make a wooden framework and cover with wire-mesh.

Greenhouses

Regularly mist-spray smooth-surfaced houseplants. Avoid dampening flowers by placing small pieces of card in front of them. If flowers become wet they soon decay, encouraging other parts to deteriorate. ▼

Calendula, a trouble-free, free-flowering annual.

Hardy annuals to sow outdoors this month where they are to flower

❀ Opium Poppy
(*Papaver somniferum*)

❀ Pheasant's Eye
(*Adonis aestivalis*)

❀ Pincushion Plant
(*Cotula barbata*)

❀ Poached Egg Plant
(*Limnanthes douglasii*)

❀ Pot Marigold
(*Calendula officinalis*)

❀ Scarlet Flax
(*Linum grandiflorum*)

❀ Snow on the Mountain
(*Euphorbia marginata*)

Biennials to sow outdoors this month in a seedbed

❀ Alpine Wallflower
(*Erysimum alpinum*)

❀ Canterbury Bell
(*Campanula medium*)

❀ Daisy
(*Bellis perennis*)

❀ Forget-me-not
(*Myosotis sylvatica*)

Organic gardening

Earthworms are essential to gardens, so do not kill them. They help aerate soil, improve drainage and assist in mixing dead plant and animal remains in the soil.

May

29

Cast not a clout ere May is out.

30

During dry periods, water plants thoroughly. Wall-trained trees especially suffer in dry periods.

31

It is still possible to sow lawn seed and to lay turves. First, however, thoroughly prepare the soil (see April)

Lilium 'Stargazer' creates a dazzling display. Keep the soil moist and mulched.

Flowers
Water and mulch lilies. Ensure the soil is moist and free from weeds before forming a mulch 5-7.5cm/2-3in thick.

Vegetables ▲
Divide chives. Remove congested plants from their pots and gently pull the soil-balls into several pieces. Discard old central parts, repotting only pieces from around the outside.

Vegetables ▲
Keep seedlings and plants free from weeds, as they encourage the presence of pests and diseases, use soil-moisture and suffocate plants. Use an onion hoe (like a miniature draw hoe) carefully to sever weeds around seedlings. Re-firm soil around plants if it is loosened.

Fruit

Inspect fruit bushes and trees regularly to check for the presence of pests and diseases. Spray immediately, adhering to the maker's instructions.

Greenhouses

Repot plants indoors and in greenhouses that fill their pots with roots. Check that their roots are free from root pests, such as Root Mealy Bugs (like small woodlice), and select a clean pot slightly larger than the present one. Gently firm potting compost around the root-ball, leaving a 12mm/½in space at the top to allow for watering.

Greenhouses

Repot chrysanthemums which will later flower in pots in greenhouses and conservatories. Stand them outdoors on a firm, well-drained surface. If plants are placed on a soft piece of ground a heavy storm might cause them to fall over.

Honesty creates a mass of fragrant, purple flowers from April to June.

Left: Hollyhocks – familiar plants in a border.

Hardy annuals to sow outdoors this month where they are to flower

❀ Stardust
   (*Gilia lutea*)

❀ Sunflower
   (*Helianthus annus*)

❀ Sweet Scabious
   (*Scabiosa atropurpurea*)

❀ Sweet Sultan
   (*Centaurea moschata*)

❀ Tassel Flower
   (*Emilia flammea*)

❀ Toadflax
   (*Linaria maroccana*)

❀ Virginian Stock
   (*Malcolmia maritima*)

Biennials to sow outdoors this month in a seedbed

❀ Foxglove
   (*Digitalis purpurea*)

❀ Hollyhock
   (*Alcea [Althaea] rosea*)

❀ Honesty
   (*Lunaria annua*)

❀ Siberian Wallflower
   (*Cheiranthus x allionii*)

❀ Wallflower
   (*Cheiranthus cheiri*)

Organic Gardening

Hedgehogs are a gardener's friend, eating slugs, beetles, cutworms and millepedes. Bread soaked in milk is a treat for them, especially in autumn when they need to gain body weight prior to hibernation.

June

This is the month of shortest nights
And garden scents are heavy and sweet
Now the rose blooms, red, pink and white
Bright, glowing in the evening heat

June

1

Calm weather in June, set corn in tune.

2

3

4

5

6

7

The risk of frost has now passed and all containers can be placed outside.

Flowers ▲
Tie up shoots of delphiniums to prevent them being damaged. Also, check other border plants to ensure they will not be damaged by wind and rain.

Lawns
When cutting grass, avoid treading on it immediately before it is cut. For safety, wear stout shoes and keep pets and children off it while it is being mown. And do not cut it when wet. If using an electric mower, start cutting at the side nearest the power source - there is then less chance of the cable being severed. And ensure a circuit-breaker is fitted into the power supply so that if the cable is cut the electricity is instantly cut off.

Vegetables
Harvest rapid-growing salad crops such as radishes and spring onions, and use the space to sow another crop that matures quickly.

Rose 'Rosy Mantle', a climbing hybrid tea.

Greenhouses
Take cuttings of regal pelargoniums, inserting them in equal parts moist peat and sharp sand.

Organic Gardening

Trap the larvae of Codling Moth as they climb trunks. Wrap strips of mutton cloth or corrugated cardboard around trunks - the larvae believe these to be safe havens in which they can overwinter. Remove and burn them in October.

Vegetables ▲
Transplant Brussels sprouts into their growing positions, 75cm/2½ft apart in rows 75-90cm/2-½-3ft apart.

Fruit
Blackberries and hybrid berries will produce new canes throughout summer.

Herbaceous perennials to sow outdoors this month in a seedbed

❀ Alpine Poppy
   (*Papaver alpinum*)

❀ Anchusa
   (*Anchusa azurea*)

❀ Cupid's Dart
   (*Catananche caerulea*)

❀ Delphinium
   (*Delphinium elatum*)

Flowers to sow this month in gentle warmth to produce plants for greenhouse and home decoration

❀ Cineraria
   (*Senecio cruentus*)

❀ Dusty Primula
   (*Primula x kewensis*)

❀ Fairy Primrose
   (*Primula malacoides*)

❀ Slipper Flower
   (*Calceolaria x herbeohybrida*)

A careful choice of garden ornaments will enhance any garden.

June

8

9

10

11

Pick strawberries as soon as they are ripe. If left on plants they soon deteriorate. Place the fruits in small baskets to avoid them being squashed.

Cut lawns regularly. The more often they are mown, the less nutrients the grass takes from the soil.

12

13

14

Remove dead flowers from plants growing in tubs, window-boxes, troughs and hanging-baskets. Cutting them off encourages the development of further flowers and smartens the display.

Vegetables ▲

Pinch out the tips of broad beans to reduce the risk of black bean aphids attacking young shoots. It also encourages plants to produce pods.

Flowers

Tidy up early-flowering rock garden plants. Removing dead leaves and flowers helps to reduce the risk of attack from slugs and snails.

Hanging baskets and garden tubs planted with a medley of summer flowers.

Herbaceous perennials to sow outdoors this month in a seedbed

- ❀ Globe Thistle
  (*Echinops ritro*)

- ❀ Granny's Bonnet
  (*Aquilegia vulgaris*)

- ❀ Iceland Poppy
  (*Papaver nudicaule*)

- ❀ Midsummer Daisy
  (*Erigeron speciosus*)

- ❀ Oriental Poppy
  (*Papaver orientale*)

Organic Gardening

Slugs devastate seedlings and other soft plants, especially when the weather is warm and wet. Slug traps are effective, but need clearing each morning. Soup-plates filled with beer and brown sugar attract these pests. Alternatively, bury wide topped milk-bottles so that their rims are level with the surrounding soil. Fill with the beer mixture. Slugs fall in and drown.

Left: Echinops, an easily grown perennial.

Below: The richly coloured Oriental Poppy.

Lawns

Feed established lawns with a quick acting lawn fertilizer at 70 grams/sq. metre (2oz/sq. yd). Ensure it is spread evenly. For large areas, wheeled fertilizer distributors speed up this job.

Greenhouses

Do not neglect to water plants. Once the compost is dry - especially if a peat-based type - it is difficult to make it again uniformly moist. At the height of summer, water plants in the morning and again during the late afternoon.

Greenhouses

Damp down greenhouses to create a moist atmosphere by mist-spraying the plants, floor and staging. Do this in early morning or by mid-afternoon, so that excess moisture disappears by nightfall. A moist atmosphere at night, when the temperature falls, encourages the presence of diseases.

June

15

16

Continue to tie new raspberry canes to supporting wires. Allow only eight canes to develop from each plant.

17

18

Water and feed tomato plants regularly, every two weeks.

19

20

21

Summer-prune gooseberries by shortening sideshoots to five leaves. This directs their vigour into the development of fruit buds.

Flowers

Water hanging-baskets regularly as the compost dries out rapidly, especially when positioned in strong sunlight. Tie the end of a hosepipe to a short cane. Water can then be dribbled into the basket without the need to stand on a stool. ▼

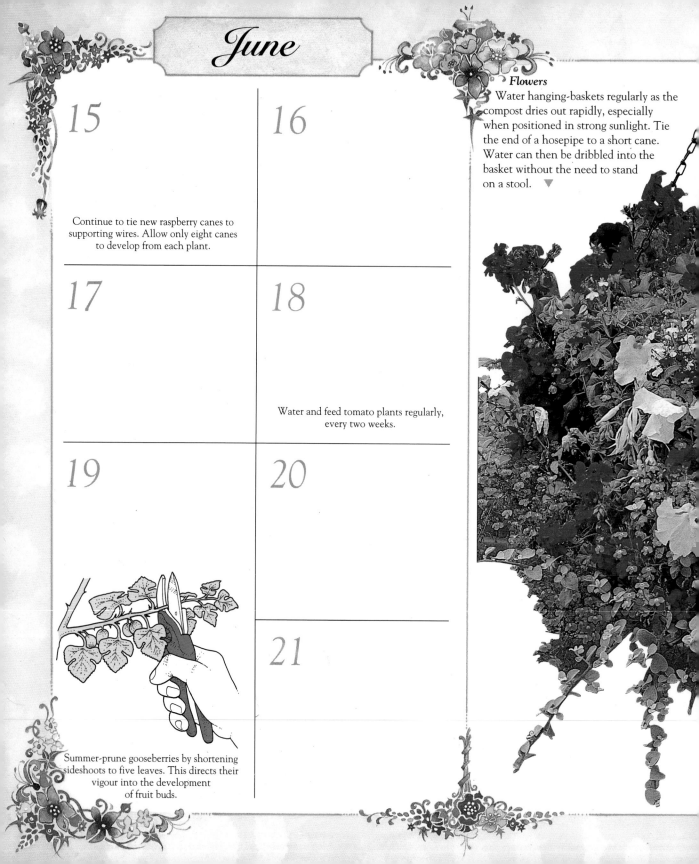

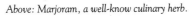

Above: Marjoram, a well-know culinary herb.

Flowers

Keep soil moist during dry periods.It is better to apply water gently over several hours than to swamp the surface in a few moments. Too much water at one time destroys the soil's structure and it just runs off the surface without penetrating to the roots. Also, apply water during evenings, not in the day when much of it would rapidly evaporate.

Flowers

Regularly check plants to ensure they are not infested with pests or diseases. At this time of year plants are quickly devastated by pests.

Flowers

Rotary grass cutters, such as strimmers, help to cut weeds and long grass under shrubs - without having to bend down.

Vegetables

Lift early potatoes. Avoid damaging the tubers - dig under them with a fork, preferably a broad-tined type. Remove soil, wash the tubers and allow to dry.

Greenhouses

Perpetual-flowering carnations are often infested by red spider mites at this time of year. In addition to spraying with pesticides, regularly mist-spray the plants. Greenfly are another pest that attacks carnations, especially around the soft tips of shoots and flower buds.

Greenhouses ▲

Take cuttings of marjoram. Water plants before taking cuttings, each 5-7.5cm/2-3in long. Remove the lower leaves and insert them in sandy compost. Water the compost to settle it around the roots and place the pot on a lightly-shaded shelf, either indoors or in a greenhouse.

Organic Gardening

Instead of using garden compost as a mulch around plants, newspapers can be used. Spread four to six thicknesses of newspaper over the soil, weighing it down with stones.

Herbaceous perennials to sow outdoors this month in a seedbed

❀ Shasta Daisy
  (*Chrysanthemum maximum*)

❀ Sweet Rocket
  (*Hesperis matronalis*)

❀ Valerian
  (*Centranthus ruber*)

❀ Yarrow
  (*Achillea filipendula*)

❀ Yarrow
  (*Achillea millefolium*)

June

22

23

Plant *Buddleia davidii*, thymes and Michaelmas Daisies to attract butterflies. ▶

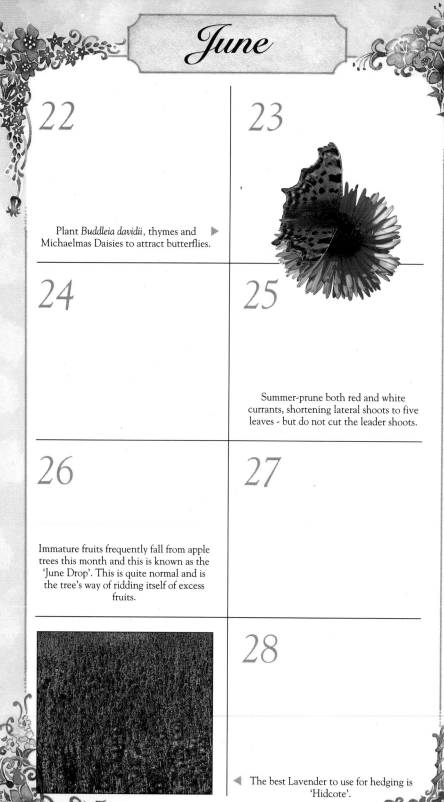

24

25

Summer-prune both red and white currants, shortening lateral shoots to five leaves - but do not cut the leader shoots.

26

27

Immature fruits frequently fall from apple trees this month and this is known as the 'June Drop'. This is quite normal and is the tree's way of ridding itself of excess fruits.

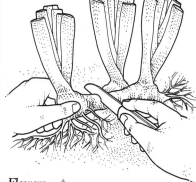

28

◀ The best Lavender to use for hedging is 'Hidcote'.

Flowers ▲
Divide congested Flag Irises as soon as their flowers fade. Lift and divide clumps, discarding the old, central part and replanting younger parts from around the outside. A sharp knife is usually necessary for this job.

Flowers
Remove sucker shoots from the bases of roses. Do not cut them off at soil-level. Instead, remove soil from around the sucker and sever close to its base.

Lawns

By this month, bare patches appear in lawns. Loosen the surface with a fork, gently re-firm and scatter lawn seed at 70 grams/sq. metre (2oz/sq. yd). Lightly water and cover with clear plastic until the seedlings are about 2.5cm/1in high.

Vegetables

Lettuce can still be sown - until late July. Sow seed 12mm/½in deep in drills 30-38cm/12-15in apart. Radishes can also be sown now.

Greenhouses

Whitefly often infests tomato plants and cinerarias. Spray or fumigate these plants, repeating the treatment ten days later to kill young whitefly that have hatched since the first treatment.

Greenhouses ▲

Large houseplants that fill their pots with roots cannot easily be repotted. Instead, gently scrape away the surface compost and replace with a fresh potting mixture, leaving space at the top so that the plant can be watered.

Above: The gloriously coloured Iris 'Brannigan' creates a splendid display in early summer.

Right: Foxgloves thrive in partial shade.

Biennials to sow outdoors this month in a seedbed

❀ Alpine Wallflower
 (*Erysimum alpinum*)

❀ Canterbury Bell
 (*Campanula medium*)

❀ Daisy
 (*Bellis perennis*)

❀ Forget-me-not
 (*Myosotis sylvatica*)

❀ Foxglove
 (*Digitalis purpurea*)

❀ Hollyhock
 (*Alcea [Althaea] rosea*)

❀ Honesty
 (*Lunaria annua*)

June

29

When cutting roses for display indoors, use sharp secateurs and sever stems just above a leaf-joint.

30

Regularly nip out the tips of shoots on houseplants grown for their foliage to encourage them to become bushy.

Rosa gallica 'Versicolor' is often know as 'Rosa Mundi'.

Flowers ▲
Increase cacti from cuttings. Sever stems at their bases, allow the cuts to dry for a couple of days and then insert into compost.

Flowers
Regularly water plants in containers, especially those in hanging-baskets. ▼

Biennials to sow outdoors this month in a seedbed

❀ Pansy
(*Viola x wittrockiana*)

❀ Siberian Wallflower
(*Cheiranthus x allionii*)

❀ Sweet William
(*Dianthus barbatus*)

❀ Wallflower
(*Cheiranthus cheiri*)

Organic Gardening

In summer there are many plants that attract clouds of butterflies. These include buddleias, marigolds, *Helichrysum bracteatum*, lobelia, mignonette, scabious, Sweet Williams, lilac and thyme.

Above: Buddleia davidii 'White Cloud'   *Below: Lobelia, a perfect edging plant.*

Lawns

Cut lawns regularly. If grass is allowed to become high, cutting is difficult and after mowing may leave yellow patches that take many weeks to regain a rich green colour. If the weather is very hot, do not cut the grass short.

Vegetables

Support peas with pea-sticks or wire-netting. Keep the plants well watered, especially when the pods start to form.

Fruit

Keep grass short in orchards, especially around young fruit trees. The grass deprives plants of nitrogen, an essential growth-promoting fertilizer for young trees.

Greenhouses

Flowers soon fall off plants in pots when the compost is allowed to become dry. Regularly check that the compost is moist - but not waterlogged.

July

A summer breeze feels like a sigh
And summer's days are long and warm
Almost every garden in July
Is rich with colour, scent and form

July

1

2

A full moon brings fair weather.

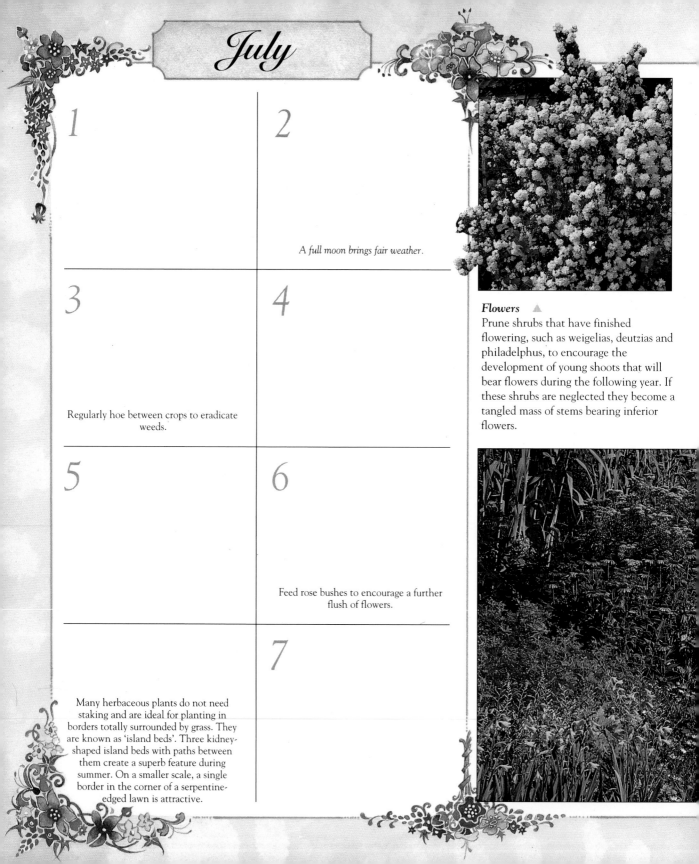

3

4

Regularly hoe between crops to eradicate weeds.

Flowers ▲
Prune shrubs that have finished flowering, such as weigelias, deutzias and philadelphus, to encourage the development of young shoots that will bear flowers during the following year. If these shrubs are neglected they become a tangled mass of stems bearing inferior flowers.

5

6

Feed rose bushes to encourage a further flush of flowers.

7

Many herbaceous plants do not need staking and are ideal for planting in borders totally surrounded by grass. They are known as 'island beds'. Three kidney-shaped island beds with paths between them create a superb feature during summer. On a smaller scale, a single border in the corner of a serpentine-edged lawn is attractive.

Flowers

Remove dead flowers to encourage plants to produce further blooms. This is especially important for plants growing in containers.

Trim hedges regularly, especially Privet. If left unclipped, they become untidy and eventually bare of shoots and leaves at their bases.

Organic Gardening

If your potatoes have been attacked by potato blight, next year use blight-resistant varieties. Potato blight is prolific in wet summers and damp weather, small brown or black spots appearing on leaves, and tubers eventually becoming a black, pulpy mess.

Lawns

Repair the edges of lawns. Cut out a section of grass, 20-25cm/8-10in wide and 38-45cm/15-18in long. Undercut this strip and reverse it so that the broken part is towards the lawn's centre. Fill up the damaged area with friable soil, firm and sow with lawn seed.

Vegetables

Transplant winter cabbages from their seedbed to cropping positions, setting them 45-60cm/18-24in apart each way.

Vegetables

Thin beetroots, carrots and lettuces. Congested plants never produce good crops.

Fruit

Protect fruits from birds by spreading nets over them, supported on metal or wooden stakes. Preferably, construct a wire fruit cage that will protect bushes and trees throughout the year.

Greenhouses

Increase large-leaved begonias such as the Rex Begonia (Begonia rex) and Iron Cross Begonia (Begonia masoniana) from leaf-cuttings. Cut the veins on the lower side and lay the leaf on moist compost, securing it in place with bent wires or small stones.

Left: A magnificent late-summer herbaceous border packed with yellow crocosmia, pink geraniums, anthemis and Purple Cone Flowers.

Right: Begonia rex, a superb houseplant.

Flowers to sow this month in gentle warmth to produce plants for greenhouse and home decoration

- ❀ Slipper Flower
  (*Calceolaria x herbeohybrida*)

- ❀ Cineraria
  (*Senecio cruentus*)

- ❀ Dusty Primula
  (*Primula x kewensis*)

- ❀ Fairy Primrose
  (*Primula malacoides*)

Herbaceous perennials to sow outdoors this month in a seedbed

- ❀ Alpine Poppy
  (*Papaver alpinum*)

- ❀ Delphinium
  (*Delphinium elatum*)

- ❀ Iceland Poppy
  (*Papaver nudicaule*)

- ❀ Midsummer Daisy
  (*Erigeron speciosus*)

July

8

9

Cut lettuces as they mature. For 'hearted' types press each lettuce's top and if firm it is ready to be cut. Use a sharp knife.

10

11

A swarm of bees in July is not worth a fly.

12

13

Cut cauliflowers when curds are mature.

14

Dogs often dig holes in lawns. Repair these by placing a piece of board, 30-38cm/12-15in square, over the hole. Use an edging-iron or spade to cut around the board, then remove the damaged turf. From an out-of-the-way area, cut a similar-sized turf and place in the hole. Firm it in place, trickle friable soil into cracks and water thoroughly.

Flowers ▲
Increase garden pinks by taking 7.5cm/3in long cuttings and inserting them in small pots of sandy compost. Place them in a cold frame or cool greenhouse.

Above: A fine group of tulips and polyanthus.

Below: Dianthus 'Whatfield Ruby'

Herbaceous perennials to sow outdoors this month in a seedbed

✿ Mullein
   (*Verbascum phoeniceum*)

✿ Oriental Poppy
   (*Papaver orientale*)

✿ Tickseed
   (*Coreopsis grandiflora*)

Organic Gardening

Chalcid wasps attack moths, butterflies and scale insects. One form is Encarsia formosa, which is especially effective at controlling greenhouse whitefly. It lays its eggs in the scale-like nymphs, which later turn black.

Flowers

Tulips heeled-in when the ground was needed for summer bedding plants can be lifted, cleaned and placed in a cool, dark, dry and vermin-proof place until replanted in autumn.

Lawns

Grass beneath children's swings soon wears out in summer - but do not replace it with concrete. Instead, either re-turf the area or place a large rubber mat under the swing.

Vegetables

Regularly water runner beans during dry periods. Mulching the soil around them with a 7.5cm/3in thick layer helps to retain moisture around their roots. But first, thoroughly water the soil.

Fruit

Plant new strawberry plants from now until mid-August, as well as in early spring. Buy plants certified free from disease. Plant them 38-45cm/15-18in apart in rows 75cm/2½ft apart. Firm soil around them and water thoroughly.

Greenhouses ▲

Do not allow coleus plants to flower. Pick them off as soon as they appear. This plant is grown for its attractive leaves.

15

Water both French beans and runner beans in dry seasons.

16

17

18

Feed air-plants by misting them with a weak - about a quarter of the normal strength - liquid fertilizer once a month from spring to late summer.

19

Bend leaves over cauliflower curds to protect them from strong sunlight.

20

21

Flowers

Keep borders free from weeds by using a hoe. Ensure the roots of perennial weeds are removed, as well as their leaves and stems.

Flowers

If left unchecked, weeds suffocate plants, rob the soil of plant foods and encourage the presence of pests and diseases.

Flowers

Late-flowering chrysanthemums in pots that have been placed outdoors will need to have their canes tied to horizontal wires to prevent them being blown over.

Lawns

Ants can be a nuisance on lawns, although usually they do little harm. However, they remove soil from around roots, which in dry weather distresses the grass. Ant repellants can be used, but ensure they are suitable for lawns.

Vegetables

Harvest Globe Artichokes when their scales are still tight. The heads at the tops of plants mature first, those on lateral shoots slightly later.

Vegetables

Harvest shallots. Gently insert a garden fork under them to loosen the soil.

Greenhouses

Pick cucumbers regularly to encourage the development of further fruits.

Greenhouses

Pot on plants as they fill their pots with roots.

Left: Chrysanthemum 'Deane Joy'

Biennials to sow this month

❀ Forget-me-not
(*Myosotis sylvatica*)

❀ Pansy
(*Viola x wittrockiana*)

Organic Gardening

Water is becoming increasingly scarce, water companies frequently banning its use in gardens. Install rain-butts to gather water from shed roofs. Also, consider re-using water from kitchens and bathrooms.

Above: Cardoons have eye-catching flowers.

July

22

23

Water soft or hairy-leaved houseplants that have become very dry by standing them in bowls shallowly filled with water. When moisture reaches the surface, remove the pot and allow excess water to drain.

24

25

Lightly trim back sage that has flowered.

26

27

Water urn plants by filling their centres with water. They can also be fed in this way, with a quarter-strength feed every three or four weeks from spring to late summer.

28

Blanch endive by loosely tying its stems together with raffia.

Flowers
Feed dahlia plants, hoeing and watering it into the soil. After thoroughly soaking the soil, form a 7.5cm/3in thick mulch around them to conserve moisture.

Flowers
Plant colchicum as soon as they can be bought, setting the corms 7.5-10cm/ 3-4in deep and in small clusters.

Flowers
Remove faded flower heads from large-flowered rhododendrons. Snap the old flower head sideways.

Vegetables
Sow turnips and swedes thinly in drills 18mm/¾in deep and in rows 38cm/15in apart. Ensure that the soil is moist.

Below: A beautifully planted urn. Be sure to keep urns and tubs well watered during hot weather. They often need watering twice a day.

Above: Colchicum speciosum creates a wonderful display from September to November. There is also a white-flowered form.

Fruit ▷

During late summer and into autumn, apples and pears will be ready for picking and storing. Now is the time to clean out the fruit store and to check that it is dry, vermin proof and well ventilated.

Greenhouses

Shade plants when the sun is shining and ventilate when the temperature rises. Spray water on the floor and staging to create a humid atmosphere.

Organic Gardening

Don't kill frogs or toads as they help to keep slugs in check. Slow-worms and hedgehogs also eat slugs.

July

29

30

31

Transplant Wallflowers, Sweet Williams and Canterbury Bells into a nursery bed to give them more space, in readiness for planting into their flowering positions in autumn. To ensure the plants transplant successfully, water both the seedlings and the nursery bed the day before they are moved.

Pinch out the growing points of dwarf beans to keep them compact.

Most houseplants like a humid atmosphere around their leaves. When displaying plants individually, moisture given off by leaves soon disperses, but when plants are in groups they create humid micro-climates.

Flowers

Disbud chrysanthemums that are not being grown as spray types. Leave the terminal buds but remove the small ones around them by bending them sideways.

Right: Chrysanthemum 'Rystar', a summer-flowering type that does not need to be disbudded. It is ideal for planting in borders in a garden.

Flowers

Increase shrubs such as escallonias, weigelas and deutzias by taking half-ripe cuttings. Insert them in equal parts moist peat and sharp sand.

Vegetables

When outdoor tomato plants have formed four trusses, pinch out the plant's growing tip. Snap this off sideways, slightly above the second leaf above the fourth truss.

Vegetables

Earth up celery grown in trenches. First, tie the stems together to prevent soil getting into their centres.

Fruit

Tidy up strawberry beds by removing old leaves and cutting off runners. Shallowly hoe between the plants.

Fruit

Increase blackberries by layering long shoots, pegging them into the soil and tying the tip to a small stake.

Organic Gardening

Green manuring helps to improve a soil's fertility and to prevent the growth of weeds. Crops such as Red Clover, Lucerne and Annual Lupins are sown and later dug into the soil.

Above: Weigela florida 'Variegata'

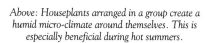

Above: Houseplants arranged in a group create a humid micro-climate around themselves. This is especially beneficial during hot summers.

August

Long afternoons in hot August
Come to thunder by and by
But then, soon after a cloudburst
The sun returns to warm and dry

August

1

Harvest Globe Artichokes when their scales are still tight.

2

3

4

Feed lawns with a slow-acting lawn fertilizer.

5

6

Gather herbs for drying.

7

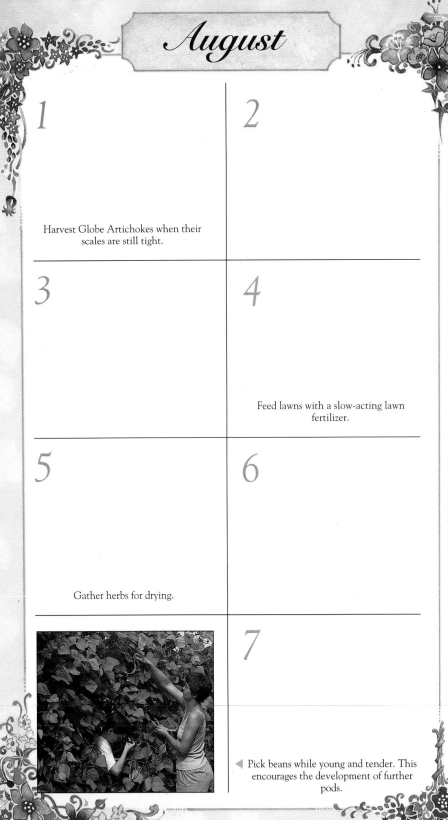

◀ Pick beans while young and tender. This encourages the development of further pods.

Flowers
Pick sweet pea flowers regularly to encourage the development of further blooms.

Vegetables
Sow spring cabbages in seedbeds, in drills 18mm/¾in deep and 15-20cm/ 6-8in apart. Later, move the young plants to a vegetable plot.

Vegetables
Lift second-early and maincrop potatoes after their leaves and stems have died down.

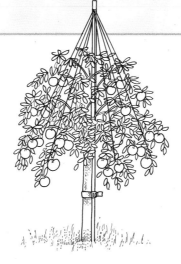

Fruit ▲

Trees heavily laden with fruit may need to have their branches supported, either with strings from a central pole or with wooden props.

Greenhouses

Remove lower leaves from tomato plants to improve air circulation and enable more light to reach the fruits.

Greenhouses

Increase Dumb Canes (*Dieffenbachia*) by cutting thick stems into pieces about 7.5cm/3in long, each containing at least one bud. Lay each piece on the surface of equal parts moist peat and sharp sand, and secure with pieces of bent wire. Cover with a domed plastic lid or plastic bag until shoots appear, then pot up individually.

Greenhouses

Pick tomatoes regularly to encourage the development of further fruits.

Below: Dumb Canes, tender plants for homes and greenhouses, have large, colourful leaves.

Above: Pick Sweet Peas regularly to encourage the development of further blooms. They are superb in gardens, as well as in flower arrangements.

Flowers to sow this month in gentle warmth to produce plants for greenhouse and home decoration

❀ Cineraria
(*Senecio cruentus*)

❀ Fairy Primrose
(*Primula malacoides*)

August

8

Pick cucumbers as they mature.

9

10

11

Remove sideshoots from tomato plants.

12

Continue to cut lawns regularly, as well as trimming the edges.

13

14

Plant bulbs of Crown Imperial (*Fritillaria imperialis*), 20cm/8in deep, from now until October.

Flowers

Cordon-grown Sweet Peas which have reached the tops of their supports can be untied, lowered, stems trailed along the ground and trained up supports further down the row.

Flowers ▶

Before going on holiday, ensure arrangements have been made to water your houseplants. Place plants in bowls shallowly filled with water, or on expanded clay particles in trays of water. Alternatively, trail the end of a capillary mat in a sink of water, the other end draped over a draining board. Plants stood on top will slowly absorb moisture by capillary action.

Vegetables

Sow turnips and swedes thinly in drills 12mm/½in deep and 30cm/12in apart. First water the drills.

Below: Crown Imperials have impressive flowers in April. Their bulbs can be planted now.

Perennials to sow outdoors this month in a seedbed

❀ Alpine Poppy
  (*Papaver alpinum*)

❀ Iceland Poppy
  (*Papaver nudicaule*)

❀ Oriental Poppy
  (*Papaver orientale*)

Organic Gardening

Check that earwigs are not attacking dahlias and chrysanthemums, chewing leaves and flowers. If noticed, place straw-packed pots upside down on bamboo canes to trap these pests at night. Every morning, remove and kill the earwigs.

Greenhouses
Dampen down greenhouses in the morning and afternoon, so that at night, when the temperature falls, there is not a humid atmosphere that would encourage the presence of diseases.

Oriental Poppies develop dominant flowers during May and June.

Vegetables
Harvest sweet corn when the tassel-like 'silks' have withered and the grains, when pressed, exude a creamy-white liquid. Harvest the cobs by pulling and twisting them downwards at the same time. ▼

August

15

16

17

18

Shallowly hoe between rows of newly-planted strawberries, severing weeds and creating a friable tilth.

19

20

21

Don't dig up plants growing wild in fields for transplanting into your garden. It is illegal. Moreover, the seeds of most of them are available from seed companies.

Lawns
Earthworms are beneficial in gardens, but in lawns they can be a problem by producing casts on the surface. These can be brushed or raked off, but if the surface becomes a mess worms can be deterred by the use of a proprietary worm deterrent.

Vegetables
Pick broad beans before the pods become tough. Also, harvest garden peas while young and tender.

Fruit
Pick apples as soon as they are ready. Cup your hand around the base of each fruit and gently lift, twisting and tilting your hand at the same time. If the stalk remains on the fruit but parts from the spur, it is ready to be picked. Treat each fruit gently as if bruised it soon deteriorates when stored.

Greenhouses
Mist spray aerial roots on houseplants such as the Swiss Cheese Plant (*Monstera deliciosa*) and philodendrons. This prevents them becoming dry and hard ▼

Annuals suitable for growing as cut-flowers for room decoration

❀ African Daisy
  (*Arctotis x hybrida*)

❀ Annual Chrysanthemum
  (*Chrysanthemum carinatum*)

❀ Chalk Flower
  (*Gypsophila elegans*)

❀ China Aster
  (*Callistephus chinensis*)

❀ Clarkia
  (*Clarkia elegans*)

❀ Coneflower
  (*Rudbeckia hirta*)

❀ Cosmea
  (*Cosmos bipinnatus*)

Organic Gardening

Rove beetles, such as the Devil's Coachhorse, live in the soil and eat mites and the pupae of Cabbage Root Flies. Both the adults and larvae of these beetles are beneficial to gardeners, and should not be destroyed.

Greenhouses
Re-pot the previous year's cyclamen that were left in their pots and placed on their sides in a greenhouse after flowering. Remove the corm and re-pot into fresh compost.

Above: Cyclamen persicum *is sold in hundreds of thousands during December. Always place them in cool rooms, away from hot fires and direct sun.*

Right: Rudbeckia fulgida 'Goldsturm' *is a perennial coneflower which flowers from July to September.*

August

22

23

Blanch cardoons. First, wrap black polythene around them.

24

25

Harvest salad onions while young.

26

27

Regularly hoe between plants. ▷

28

Lift beetroots, using a garden fork to ease them from the soil.

Flowers

Increase the Mexican Hat (*Kalanchoe daigremontiana*) and Chandelier Plant (*Kalanchoe tubiflora*) by removing the young plantlets that grow on their leaves and pressing them into moist compost. When rooted, pot them up into small pots.

Flowers

Attractive indoor features can be created by securing small bromeliads to a branch, about 90cm-1m/3-3¼ft long, fixed vertically in a large pot or small tub. Regularly mist-spray plants, especially during their establishment.

Vegetables

The acidity or alkalinity of soil can be assessed by using a simple soil-testing kit. Mix a random sample of soil with chemicals, creating a colour that when compared with a colour chart indicates the soil's pH. The degree of acidity shows the amount of lime needed. Never use lime at the same time as applying manure or compost. Indeed, it is best to dig soil and incorporate organic material, then later to apply lime.

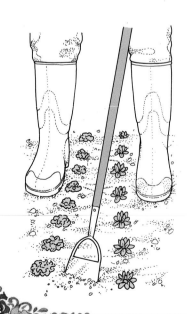

Above: Nemesia, one of the jewels in a garden, forms a superb display from June to August.

Right: Godetias are hardy annuals with flowers from June to August.

Organic Gardening

It is surprising how much money can be saved each year by recycling supporting wires, canes, poles, boxes and string. As crops are harvested or die, clean their supports and store in a shed.

Fruit

Blackcurrants planted the previous autumn or early in the year will have developed young shoots from their bases. Cut out at soil-level the weakest of these. Shoots that are left will produce fruit during the following year.

Greenhouses ▷

When growing houseplants with aerial roots, provide them with a moss-covered pole so that moisture is retained to keep them soft and pliable.

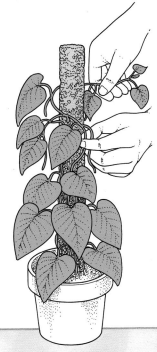

Annuals suitable for growing as cut-flowers for room decoration

❋ Godetia
   (*Godetia grandiflora*)

❋ Love-in-a-Mist
   (*Nigella damascena*)

❋ Love-lies-bleeding
   (*Amaranthus caudatus*)

❋ Mallow
   (*Lavatera trimestris*)

❋ Mignonette
   (*Reseda odorata*)

❋ Nasturtium
   (*Tropaeolum majus*)

❋ Nemesia
   (*Nemesia strumosa*)

August

29

30

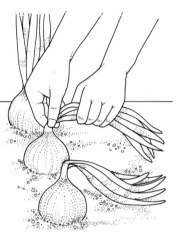

Bend over the tops of onions in
preparation for lifting them.

31

Flowers
Disbud chrysanthemums that are not
being grown as spray varieties. Leave the
terminal bud and gently remove the
small buds from around it. Bend them
sideways.

Vegetables
Harvest kohlrabi when the size of tennis
balls.

Vegetables
Harvest runner beans while they are
young and tender. If left, they become
tough and stringy.

Fruit
In dry seasons it is necessary to water
soft-fruit bushes and plants, especially
newly-planted strawberries. Ensure that
the soil is thoroughly soaked, not just the
surface lightly moistened.

Greenhouses
Check that greenhouse shading, earlier
painted on the glass, has not been
washed off. Direct sunlight at this time
can be too strong for many plants.

*Below: African Violets can be easily propagated
by inserting leaf-cuttings in moist peat and sharp
sand. Insert them in hormone rooting powder.*

Increase African Violets by cutting off a
few healthy leaves, complete with their
stems (petioles). Dip the ends of their
short stems in a hormone rooting powder
and insert three in a 7.5cm/3in wide pot
containing equal parts moist peat and
sharp sand. Do not position them nearer
than 12mm/½in to the pot's edge, as if
watering is neglected this is where the
compost first becomes dry. When rooted,
pot up individually into small pots of
peat-based compost.

Annuals suitable for growing as cut-flowers for room decoration

❀ Pot Marigold
  (*Calendula officinalis*)

❀ Scabious
  (*Scabiousa atropurpurea*)

❀ Star of the Veldt
  (*Dimorphotheca aurantiaca*)

❀ Sunflower
  (*Helianthus annuus*)

❀ Tassel Flower
  (*Emilia flammea*)

❀ Tickseed
  (*Coreopsis calliopsis*)

❀ Toadflax
  (*Linaria maroccana*)

❀ Zinnia
  (*Zinnia elegans*)

Left: Kohlrabi will be ready to harvest this month, when the size of tennis balls.

Below: Zinnias are superb in flower arrangements, as well as in borders.

Greenhouses

Increase the Jade Plant (*Crassula argentea*) by pulling off a few leaves, allowing the surfaces to dry for a few days and then inserting them in equal parts moist peat and sharp sand. Position them out of direct sunlight. When rooted, pot up the leaves individually.

Organic Gardening

Ground beetles, such as the Violet Ground Beetle, live in the soil, eating soft-tissued grubs and adult pests, including slugs and cabbage rootfly eggs. Therefore, do not kill them.

September

September fruits are on the bough
And the bright apple is king of all
Red, golden, russet - brimming now
Ripe for the picking before they fall

September

1

2

*September blow soft,
Till the fruit's in the loft.*

3

4

Sow winter lettuces and winter spinach.

5

6

*Harvest potatoes on ground where
wireworms are troublesome.*

7

Pull up dead summer-bedding plants in
preparation for planting spring-flowering
bulbs. Fork the soil and add a light
dressing of bonemeal.

Flowers ▲
Lift gladioli plants that have flowered.
Gently push a garden fork under the
plants and lift the corms complete with
their stems. If the stems have withered
they can be easily removed from the
corms. If not, tie up the stems and hang
in a cool, airy shed until the foliage dies.

Flowers
Prune rambler roses. Untie them from
their supports, lay them on the ground
and cut out at ground-level all stems that
have borne flowers. Retain shoots made
during the current season and tie them
to the supports.

Fruit
Continue to pick apples, as soon as their
stalks part easily from the fruiting spurs.
Each stalk must remain attached to its
fruit. Also, pick pears as soon as their
stalks readily part from the spurs.

Fruit
Cut out at soil level raspberry canes that
bore fruit earlier in the year. Space out
the young canes and tie them to their
supports.

Greenhouses
Continue to train shoots of the Pink
Jasmine (*Jasminum polyanthum*) around a
hoop, taking care not to kink the stems.
It flowers in greenhouses and indoors
from November to April, bearing
scented, white and pale pink flowers.

Greenhouses ▲

Prick out cyclamen seedlings that have developed from seeds sown in August.

Above: Aster amellus produces a colourful display.

Left: Day Lilies flower mainly from June to August, and often into early September.

Herbaceous perennials for growing as cut-flowers for room decoration

❀ Aster
(*Aster amellus*)

❀ Baby's Breath
(*Gypsophila paniculata*)

❀ Bear's Breeches
(*Acanthus mollis*)

❀ Blanket Flower
(*Gaillardia aristata*)

❀ Day Lily
(*Hemerocallis*)

❀ Delphinium
(*Delphinium elatum*)

Organic Gardening

Leatherjackets and chafer grubs are frequently a problem on lawns in late summer and autumn. To check their presence, one evening place a damp sack over part of the lawn. Grubs that are present will be seen under the sack in the morning - remove and destroy them. If the infestation is severe, water the lawn and place a large piece of black polythene over the area. In the morning, remove and pick off the grubs.

September

8

Trim off the largest leaves from parsley to encourage the growth of fresh ones.

9

10

11

Use ground limestone when liming soil in autumn and winter - order it now.

12

Place cloches over outdoor tomato plants to help ripen the last fruits. First, cut the plants from their supports and lay them in a row.

13

14

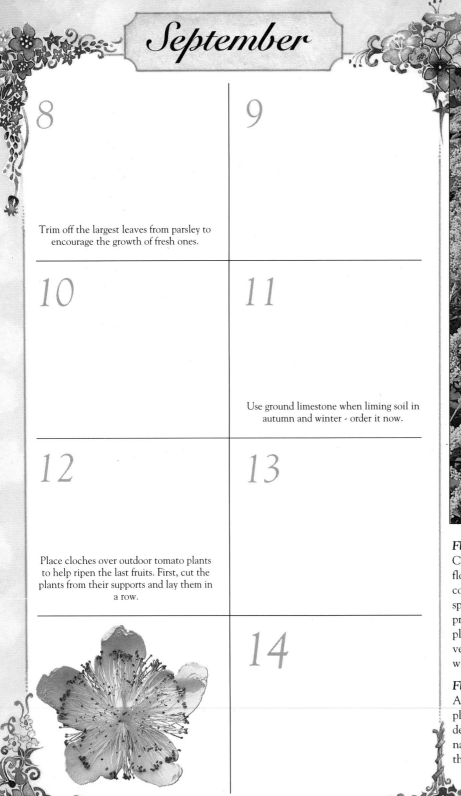

Flowers
Cut down herbaceous plants that have flowered and look a mess. However, in cold areas leave this job until early spring. The stems provide some protection for the roots of delicate plants. Additionally, these stems look very attractive in winter when covered with frost.

Flowers
As soon as daffodil bulbs can be bought, plant them in holes about 13cm/5in deep. In flower beds use a trowel, but if naturalized in grass a bulb-planting tool that removes a core of grass and soil is better. Place a bulb in each hole and replace the turf.

Organic Gardening

Using peat in the garden and greenhouse is not environmentally friendly as it helps in the destruction of peat bogs, the natural habitats of many animals, insects, birds and plants. Instead, use materials based on coir-dust, a waste product from the coconut industry.

Herbaceous perennials for growing as cut-flowers for room decoration

* Fleabane
  (*Erigeron speciosus*)

* Foxtail Lily
  (*Eremurus rubustus*)

* Giant Bellflower
  (*Campanula latifolia*)

* Globe Flower
  (*Trollium x hybridus*)

* Globe Thistle
  (*Echinops humilis*)

* Golden Rod
  (*Solidago*)

Left: The spectacular Foxtail Lily, which grows over head-height, needs sun and protection from cold winds. Divide clumps in autumn.

Below: Mother-in-Law's Tongue is a spectacular plant for the home and greenhouse. It is ideal for positioning on sunny windowsills.

Vegetables
Plant spring cabbages 25-30cm/10-12in apart in rows 30cm/12in apart. A few weeks later, draw a little soil around their bases to give protection from frost.

Greenhouses
Complete the harvesting of melons and clear away the plants.

Greenhouses ▷
Divide a congested Mother-in-Law's Tongue (*Sansevieria trifasciata*). Carefully remove the pot and gently pull apart the soil-ball and roots to form several plants. Repot each part into a fresh pot and compost.

September

15

16

Don't re-use potting or seed compost - the nutrients will have been exhausted and it may contain pests and diseases.

Flowers ▲
Cut off seed-heads from Honesty (*Lunaria annua*), Chinese Lanterns (*Physalis alkekengi*) and poppies for decoration indoors in winter.

Lawns
Aerating lawns is best tackled in autumn and early winter. Equipment to remove cores of soil from lawns can be bought or hired and are ideal for large areas. Small lawns, however, are usually aerated by inserting the prongs of garden forks into them. After forking, rake the lawn and brush in a mixture of equal parts sharp sand and potting compost.

17

18

Tie up the leaves of endive and place a large pot over them to blanch their stems. Block off the hole in the pot's top to exclude all light.

19

20

21

◄ Plant outdoor bulbs such as crocuses, muscari, daffodils, narcissus, Snowdrops and Winter Aconites. ▶

Above: The brightly faced Leopard's Bane.

Vegetables

As soon as crops are harvested, remove the debris so that the soil's surface is bare. Rubbish left on the soil encourages pests and diseases to linger and spread. Rubbish known to be contaminated with pests or diseases should be burned.

Greenhouses ▶

A novel way to grow hyacinth bulbs for indoor decoration is in bulb-glasss. Fill a bulb glass to its neck with clean water, then put a bulb on top. Place it in a cool, dry, frost-proof shed or cellar until the bulb's roots are 10cm/4in long and shoots 2.5cm/1in out of the neck. Then move indoors and gradually increase the temperature to 18°C/64°F.

Greenhouses

Move large exhibition chrysanthemums, currently growing outdoors in pots, into a greenhouse where they will flower.

Herbaceous perennials for growing as cut-flowers for room decoration

❀ Helenium
   (*Helenium autumnale*)

❀ Heliopsis
   (*Heliopsis scabra*)

❀ Jerusalem Cross
   (*Lychnis chalcedonica*)

❀ Leopard's Bane
   (*Doronicum*)

❀ Lily-of-the-Valley
   (*Convallaria majalis*)

❀ Masterwort
   (*Astrantia*)

Organic Gardening

Hoverflies characteristically 'hover' in mid-air. A few are pests, but some voraciously feed on aphids. A single hoverfly has been known to eat twenty-one aphids in twenty minutes, while each larva destroys up to 900 aphids in its lifetime.

Lily-of-the-Valley flowers during April and May.

September

22

23

Always wear safety goggles when using chain-saws, strimmers and hedge-clippers.

24

25

When clearing a garden pond in late summer and autumn, make the job easier by placing a ladder or long plank over it.

26

27

Check that greenhouse ventilators close properly. During hot summers, wooden ones frequently become distorted and subsequenty in winter allow draughts to enter the greenhouse.

28

Freesias that have been in a cold frame must now be taken into a greenhouse. Water the compost and give the plants plenty of light and air.

Flowers
Prepare ground for the planting of herbaceous plants. In cold areas, this task is best left until spring.

Lawns
Bumps and depression in lawns can be eliminated by slicing back the turf and either adding or removing soil.

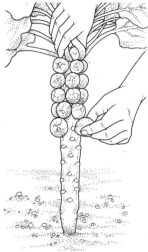

Vegetables
Pick Brussels sprouts as soon as the buttons are firm. Pick only those that are ready, leaving the others to mature.

Above: Crocuses can be planted this month.

Herbaceous perennials for growing as cut-flowers for room decoration

❀ Michaelmas Daisy
 (*Aster novi-belgii*)

❀ Monkshood
 (*Aconitum napellus*)

❀ Peruvian Lily
 (*Alstroemeria ligtu hybrids*)

❀ Phlox
 (*Phlox paniculata*)

❀ Pyrethrum
 (*Pyrethrum roseum*)

Michaelmas Daisies are excellent as cut flowers, as well as for brightening borders in autumn.

Fruit

Plant hybrid berries and blackberries from now until late winter. Space the plants 1.8-3m/6-10ft apart, depending on the variety's vigour. After planting, cut the canes down to about 23cm/9in high. Now is the time to either check their supporting wires or to provide new ones - it is easier to do this job when plants are small. Provide wires, strained between strong end-posts, 30cm/12in, 75cm/2½ft and 1.5m/5ft above the soil.

Greenhouses

Pot up crocuses (*Crocus chrysanthus*) in late summer. However, unlike daffodils, hyacinths and tulips, which can be given high temperatures and 'forced' into flower, crocuses cannot. Pot-up top-sized corms in a pot with holes in its sides and top, using either bulb-fibre or gritty compost. Water the compost and place the pot in a black polythene bag in a cool, frost-proof shed or cellar. When shoots are 2.5cm/1in high, move indoors into a cool room. Keep the compost moist - and avoid high temperatures.

Organic Gardening

Green lacewings appear delicate, but are voracious eaters of aphids and other small, soft-bodied insects.

September

29

30

Always clean garden tools after use and oil bright-metal parts. It extends their lives.

Flowers

Remove early flowers from winter-flowering pansies to encourage the development of larger blooms later in the season.

Flowers

Protect choice alpine plants by placing small cloches or pieces of glass over them. This gives protection from rain. Alpines survive low temperatures, but a combination of water and frost soon kills them.

Pot up daffodil bulbs in late summer and autumn, setting them slightly apart and with their noses just above the surface of the compost. Water the compost, allow excess moisture to drain and place the pot in a black plastic bag. Place these in a cool shed or cellar. Periodically, check the compost to ensure it is slightly moist, and when shoots are 10cm/4in high move indoors and place in a cool position. Slowly increase the temperature from 7°C/45°F to 15°C/59°F. Keep the compost moist.

Lawns

Dismantle, clean and pack up garden swings, chairs, tables and children's playthings from lawns and patios. Either place them in a shed or tie a large plastic sheet over them.

Vegetables

Harvest haricot beans when the pods turn yellow. Also, cut marrows before the end of the month.

Vegetables ▶

Asparagus crowns planted in April will now have produced tall shoots and fern-like leaves. Cut these down to soil level and lightly fork between the rows so that soil is left in a slight ridge.

Greenhouses

Check the heating system. If electric, ensure it is safe and that a current-breaker device is installed. If a paraffin heater is used, clean wicks and buy fuel in preparation for low temperatures.

Organic Gardening

There are many flowers that attract butterflies in late summer and autumn, such as Michaelmas Daisies, *(Ceratostigma willmottianum)*, chrysanthemums, Ice Plant *(Sedum spectabile)* and heleniums.

Many late summer-flowering plants attract butterflies, such as the Small Tortoiseshell. Position these plants in a warm, wind-free area.

Herbaceous perennials for growing as cut-flowers for room decoration

❀ Sea Lavender
(Limonium latifolium)

❀ Shasta Daisy
(Chrysanthemum maximum)

❀ Sneezewort
(Achillea ptarmica)

❀ Tickseed
(Coreopsis grandiflora)

❀ Yarrow
(Achillea filipendula)

October

Autumn tones shine on the trees
And October days are growing short
Now the garden's bright with leaves
In the fading sunlight caught

October

1

2

Cut off and burn old potato shoots badly infected with diseases.

3

4

Encourage green tomatoes to ripen by wrapping them in paper and placing in drawers.

5

6

7

◀ Tie onions into 'ropes' as a way to store them. Hang them in a cool, dry store.

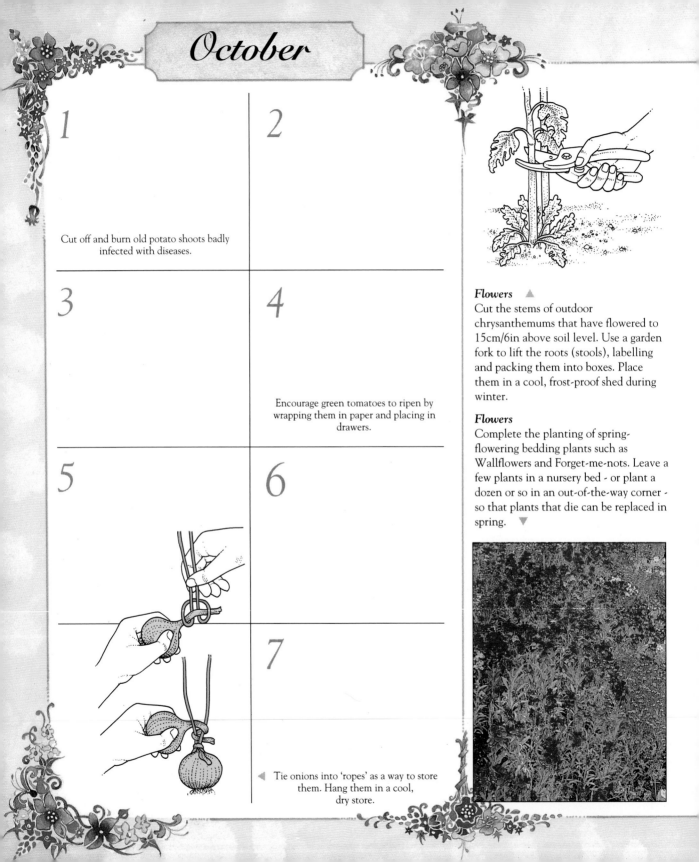

Flowers ▲
Cut the stems of outdoor chrysanthemums that have flowered to 15cm/6in above soil level. Use a garden fork to lift the roots (stools), labelling and packing them into boxes. Place them in a cool, frost-proof shed during winter.

Flowers
Complete the planting of spring-flowering bedding plants such as Wallflowers and Forget-me-nots. Leave a few plants in a nursery bed - or plant a dozen or so in an out-of-the-way corner - so that plants that die can be replaced in spring. ▼

October is a good month for greenhouse maintenance.

Lawns
After naturalizing daffodils in a lawn, mark out the area so that it is not walked on.

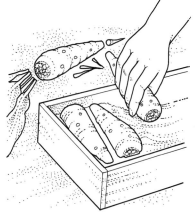

Vegetables ▲
Dig up chicory when their leaves die. Cut off their roots and store them in a cellar or cool shed. The roots are later forced to produce fresh shoots known as chicons.

Fruit
Plant blackcurrants from now and until early spring, whenever the soil is workable. Do not plant them when the soil is frozen or waterlogged. Space the plants 1.5-1.8m/5-6ft apart, immediately cutting down the shoots to within 5cm/2in of the soil's surface.

Herbaceous perennials that produce seed heads for room decoration in winter

- ❀ Baby's Breath
  (*Gypsophila paniculata*)

- ❀ Bear's Breeches
  (*Acanthus mollis/A. spinosus*)

- ❀ Burning Bush
  (*Dictamnus albus*)

Greenhouses
Ventilate greenhouses whenever possible to prevent the build up of stagnant air and high humidity, which may encourage the presence of diseases.

Greenhouses
Scrub off shading from the outsides of greenhouses. Thoroughly spray the outside with clean water. Also, take down and store roller blinds.

Organic Gardening
Don't store potatoes in plastic bags as they create condensation and cause tubers to decay. Preferably, use hessian sacks. Alternatively, employ sacks made from several layers of brown paper. Store them in a cool, frost-proof shed, and cover with an old blanket to exclude light.

October

8

9

Unless the weather is exceptionally mild, do not trim hedges between now and April.

10

11

When harvesting trench celery, first use a trowel to remove soil from around their bases, then a garden fork to lever the roots out of the soil. Take care not to damage the stems.

12

13

Feed cyclamen plants with a weak liquid fertilizer every two weeks. ▶

14

When digging vegetable plots this autumn and winter, do not remove stones. They help to maintain a good soil structure, improve drainage and keep the soil moist in summer.

Flowers
Remove stakes and canes that were used to support plants during summer. Brush off soil, wash them with a disinfectant and store in a dry shed.

Flowers
Half-ripe cuttings of shrubs - taken earlier in the year and inserted in equal parts moist peat and sharp sand - will now have produced roots. Pot them individually into small pots and place in a cold frame or cold greenhouse during winter.

Lawns
If autumn has been exceptionally wet, badly-drained lawns will now be evident, with water resting on the surface. Install drains now or during winter. Dig narrow trenches in a herringbone fashion, with the end draining into a ditch or large hole filled with rubble. Use either tiles butted together or a trench filled with rubble.

Vegetables

Plant spring cabbages 25-30cm/10-12in apart in rows 30cm/12in apart.

Fruit

Plant raspberry canes from now until early spring. Dig the soil and mix in well-decayed manure or garden compost. Plant the canes 45cm/1½ft apart in rows 1.8m/6ft apart. Ensure that each cane is covered by about 7.5cm/3in of soil. Then, cut down the stems to 30-38cm/12-15in high.

Greenhouses

Pot up tulip bulbs in late summer and autumn, close together and with their noses covered with compost. Water the compost, place the pot in a black polythene bag and put in a cold, frost-proof shed or cellar. When shoots are 5cm/2in high, move indoors into 7-10°C/45-50°F. Later, when shoots are 10cm/4in high, raise the temperature to 18°C/64°F.

Herbaceous perennials that produce seed heads for room decoration in winter

❀ Butterfly Iris
  (*Iris ochroleuca*)

❀ Cardoon
  (*Cynara cardunculus*)

❀ Chinese Lantern
  (*Physalis alkekengi*)

❀ Delphinium
  (*Delphinium elatum*)

Organic Gardening

Growing-bags that grew vegetables this year need not be thrown away at the end of the season. Instead, store them in a dry shed and next spring top up with peat (or, preferably, with an alternative to peat) and add a sprinkling of a general fertilizer. Plant summer-flowering bedding plants in them.

Delphinium elatum *has spire-like flower heads.*

Left: Tulip bulbs can be planted this month.

October

15

16

Lift self-blanching celery for storing.

17

18

Water greenhouse plants only in the morning, so that by nightfall the atmosphere is dry.

19

20

21

Don't feed houseplants in winter unless they are active or flowering. Pot plants which are fed when dormant become soft and prone to pests and diseases.

Flowers ▲
Lift dahlia tubers as soon as their leaves have been blackened by frost. Cut off their stems, about 13cm/5in above soil-level, and carefully dig up the tubers, taking care not to damage them. Wipe off the soil and place them upside down in boxes to dry out. Put them in a cool, dry, frost-proof shed. Label each plant.

Lawns
Prepare the ground for new lawns. Dig the area and remove all perennial weeds. Leave the surface with large lumps of soil exposed to the weathering action of winter weather. Prepare an area slightly larger than that required - the edges can be cut back after establishment. In spring, rake the surface level.

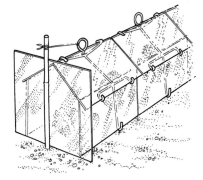

Vegetables

Produce winter spinach by placing cloches over late sowings. Place sheets of glass at the ends of the tunnel.

Vegetables

Sow lettuce seeds under cloches or in cold frames by the end of this week, in shallow drills about 15cm/6in apart. About the middle of December, transplant the young plants into frames or cloches, setting them 30cm/12in apart each way.

Greenhouses

In autumn and winter, giving plants in pots the precise amount of water they need is difficult. This is because plants that are not actively growing do not need much water. Conversely, if too little water is given leaves become dry and crisp.

Above: Lamb's Ears – a descriptively named perennial.

Below: The Giant Lily is only suitable for growing in large gardens.

Herbaceous perennials that produce seed heads for room decoration in winter

❀ Giant Lily
   (*Cardiocrinum giganteum*)

❀ Globe Thistle
   (*Echinop humilis*)

❀ Lamb's Tongue
   (*Stachys byzantina/S. lanata*)

❀ Oriental Poppy
   (*Papaver orientale*)

October

22

23

Plant rhubarb crowns from now until November.

24

25

Examine stored vegetables and remove those showing signs of decay.

26

27

Continue to clear up the garden, composting soft materials but burning those contaminated with pests and diseases.

28

Flowers ▲

Clean-up garden ponds, removing dead plants as well as leaves that have fallen in. If there are still large numbers of leaves to fall from nearby trees, place a net or wire-netting over the pond. Rubbish that remains in the pond decomposes, creating gases detrimental to fish.

Lawns ▶

Rake up leaves. If left on a lawn they decompose and worms pull them into the soil. Sweep the leaves into heaps and use two boards, each about 30cm/12in long and 20cm/8in wide, to lift them into a wheelbarrow.

Herbaceous perennials that produce seed heads for room decoration in winter

- ❀ Ornamental Thistle
  (*Onopordon acanthium*)

- ❀ Paeony
  (*Paeonia mlokosewitschii*)

- ❀ Pearl Everlasting
  (*Anaphalis triplinervis*)

- ❀ Sea Holly
  (*Eryngium maritimum*)

Organic Gardening

If compost is in short supply next year for mulching plants, consider the use of black polythene. The life-span of polythene depends on its thickness - cheap bin-liner bags last for only one season. Other mulching materials include carpets, cardboard and newspapers.

Fruit

Plant red and white currant bushes from now until early spring, setting them 1.5m/5ft apart. ▼

Fruit

Increase blackcurrants by forming 20cm/8in long cuttings from shoots produced earlier in the year. Insert them 15cm/6in deep in a nursery-bed.

October

29

30

Leaves fall off bougainvilleas that are exposed to sudden drops in temperature. Reposition them in 10°C/50°F.

31

In autumn and winter, chain-saws are frequently used to cut trees and branches. Safety is essential, as if misused a chain-saw is a lethal weapon.

- Wear protective goggles.
- Wear a thick jacket with sleeves.
- Don't wear loose clothing or a scarf.
- Don't use the saw above waist height.
- Don't use in rain or on wet wood.
- Keep away from children and animals.
- Don't insert the chain into a previous cut.
- If electrically powered, ensure a circuit breaker is fitted into the power supply.

The peeling bark of Acer griseum.

Flowers

Most houseplant enthusiasts judge if plants need water by looking at the compost or by rubbing a thumb over its surface. If the compost's surface is light coloured it indicates that water is needed. Alternatively, tap clay pots with a cotton-reel attached to a cane. If it produces a ringing note, water is needed. If it creates a dull sound, the compost is sufficiently moist.

Lawns

Ensure that plants in borders alongside lawns are not overlapping the grass and causing it to die.

Fruit

Increase both red and white currants by taking 30cm/1ft long cuttings from shoots produced during the current year. Remove all but the top four buds on each cutting and insert them 15cm/6in deep in a nurserybed.

Greenhouses

If one of the sides of your greenhouse is exposed to cold north winds, spread and secure a sheet of clear plastic over it. In exposed areas, long-term protection can be provided by planting a windbreak on the north and east side - but not too close to the greenhouse. Additionally, insulative material can be fixed to the inside of the greenhouse.

Organic Gardening

Electric-powered shredders are popular and can be hired from tool shops. They are ideal for creating mulching material from woody garden waste. Wear protective goggles when using them.

Above: Vitis coignetiae *reveals beautifully coloured leaves in autumn.*

Left: Stinking Iris, whose seed heads make striking indoor arrangements in autumn.

Herbaceous perennials that produce seed heads for room decoration in winter

❀ Sea Lavender
   (*Limonium latifolium*)

❀ Stinking Iris
   (*Iris foetidissima*)

❀ Yarrow
   (*Achillea filipendula*)

Greenhouses

To give plants better light, put them on shelves in the roof. However, such places are where the temperature decreases most dramatically at night.

November

Clear November skies are rare
As like as not fierce storms arrive
But still the garden is not bare
Chrysanthemums the rain survive

November

1

2

Winter is summer's heir.

3

Lift parsnips for storing. Also, dig up winter cabbages: cut off the stumps and place their heads on shelves in a dry, airy shed.

4

Give celery plants a final earthing.

5

6

Clear old runner bean stems and leaves and place them on a compost heap.

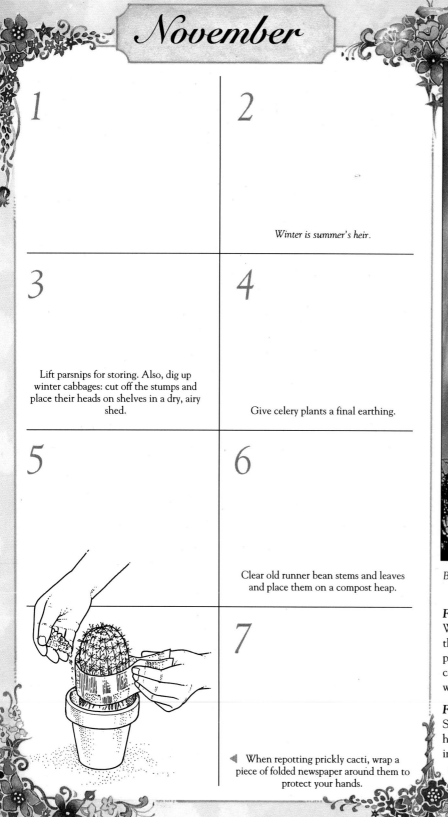

7

◀ When repotting prickly cacti, wrap a piece of folded newspaper around them to protect your hands.

Bonfires present a good opportunity to burn garden rubbish, especially plants infected by diseases.

Flowers
When preparing new flower borders, dig the soil 30cm/12in deep and mix in plenty of well-decayed manure or garden compost. Remove and burn all perennial weeds.

Flowers
Spring-flowering bedding plants that have not been planted in formal beds or in pots and tubs on patios can be set around shrubs to create extra colour in spring.

Greenhouses

Protect plants in cold frames by covering them on frosty nights with hessian. Roll it back in the morning, as soon as the frost has gone.

Vegetables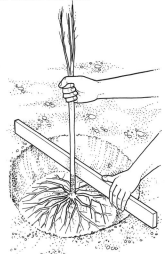

Cut globe artichokes down to soil level and cover the roots with straw to protect them from severe frost.

Lawns

Lawn cutting is probably over for this year, so thoroughly clean the mower. Scrape off soil and old grass-cuttings, wash the mower and wipe dry. Cover all metal parts with a thin layer of oil or grease, then place the mower in a dry, well-aerated shed. Have electrical parts checked by a competent electrician.

Fruit

Plant gooseberry bushes from now and until early spring, whenever the soil is workable. Space the bushes 1.5m/5ft apart.

Fruit ▲

Plant bare-rooted fruit trees from now and until late spring, whenever the soil is not frozen or waterlogged. Dig a large hole and use a fork to loosen the soil in its base, forming it into a slight mound. Place the tree in position, with its roots spread out over the mound. Check its depth by placing a piece of wood across the hole. The old soil mark on the stem should be about 2.5cm/1in below the surface. Replace soil around the roots, gently lifting the tree several times to ensure soil trickles between them. Firm the soil.

Organic Gardening ▲

A few birds are pests of fruit trees, but some kill the grubs of pests. These birds can be encouraged into your garden by planting shrubs that provide food for them, such as berberis, hawthorn, holly, Rowan, Sea Buckthorn, Spindle, Wayfaring Tree and Yew.

November

8

Rake up leaves and place them on a compost heap. If left on paths they become a hazard.

9

10

11

Protect late cauliflowers from frost by bending one or two leaves over the curds.

12

13

Harvest leeks by using a garden fork to dig them up. Trim off roots and remove soil.

14

Inspect lawns and remove firework debris that remains from Guy Fawkes night festivities. If left, it becomes trodden into the lawn.

Flowers

Compost in large tubs often becomes too wet in winter when shrubs and small trees in them are dormant. Place two bricks on the compost around the plant's stem, then cover with clear plastic. The bricks raise the plastic and ensure water drains towards the outside of the tub and not to its centre. Remove this covering in late winter.

Flowers ▲

Agapanthus growing in tubs needs protection from frost. Cover the plants with 10cm/4in of straw.

Greenhouses

In winter, water plants in greenhouses very carefully. If plants are excessively watered their roots die and the foliage wilts. If you are doubtful about a plant needing water, leave it alone. Keeping the compost slightly dry in winter is better that excessive watering, but ensure that flowering plants are regularly watered.

Organic Gardening

Open compost heaps attract rats, especially in winter when kitchen scraps are added to them. If you see a rat, contact your local pest control officer. Over 50 percent of rats carry the bacteria that causes Weil's disease, which can affect humans, dogs and cats. Humans are infected through open cuts and abrasions. Moist soil and compost heaps are a risk if visited by rats, so wear rubber gloves or gauntlets.

Below: The sweetly scented Lily-of-the-Valley has crowns that can be potted this month for flowering in spring.

Greenhouses △

When planting a terrarium, first arrange the plants on a piece of paper shaped like the container's base. At the same time, wipe smooth-surfaced leaves and brush off dust from hairy ones.

Greenhouses

Cut down to 20cm/8in high chrysanthemum plants that have finished flowering in greenhouses. Burn the leaves and woody stems. Ensure that each pot is labelled and keep the compost barely damp.

Everlasting flowers to raise from seeds for room decoration in winter

- ❀ Cudweed
  (*Gnaphalum* 'Fairy Gold')

- ❀ Everlasting
  (*Helipterum manglesii*)

- ❀ Everlasting
  (*Helipterum roseum*)

- ❀ Globe Amaranth
  (*Gomphrena globosa*)

Greenhouses

Pot up the crowns of Lily of the Valley (*Convallaria majalis*) to encourage early flowering. Put a few crowns in a 15cm/6in wide pot, using equal parts sharp sand and loam-based potting compost. Lightly cover the crowns with compost, water them and stand the pots in a cool position. Keep the compost moist but not waterlogged.

November

15

16

In cold areas, where rose pruning is best left until early spring, shorten top growth now by about a third to reduce the risk of damage from strong winds.

17

18

Greenhouse paths invariable become worn down, slabs subsiding or tilting. Now is the time to reposition them.

19

20

Greenhouses ▲
When planting a carboy, use a tube of rolled card to ensure compost does not dirty the container's sides when filling it.

Flowers
Plant bare-rooted trees and shrubs from now until early spring, whenever the soil is not frozen or waterlogged. Container-grown plants, however, can be planted at anytime, whenever the soil is workable.

Flowers ▷
Plant deciduous hedges formed from bare-rooted plants from now and until early spring. Trim back excessively long or damaged roots, and after planting cut the plants back by about half to encourage shoots to develop from their bases. If this job is neglected the hedge will have gaps along its base.

21

Prune established apple trees between now and late winter.

Everlasting flowers to raise from seeds for room decoration in winter

- ❀ Honesty
  (*Lunaria annua*)

- ❀ Immortelle
  (*Xeranthemum annuum*)

- ❀ Matricaria
  (*Matricaria grandiflora*)

- ❀ Paper Daisies
  (*Lawrencellia*)

Lawns

When digging borders alongside lawns, place a plank on the turf to prevent its edges being broken. Also, if you intend to run a wheelbarrow off the grass and on to the border, use planks to build up the height of the border.

The delicate-looking seed heads of Honesty.

Vegetables

Continue to pick Brussels sprouts as soon as their buttons are firm. Also, harvest parsnips, using a garden fork to ease them from the ground. Remove all soil before taking them indoors.

Greenhouses

Encourage African Violets (*Saintpaulia ionantha*) to develop roots by suspending the ends of their leaf stalks (petioles) in water. Fill a small bottle with clean water, wrap a piece of paper over the top, pierce a hole in it and push a leaf stalk through, so that its end is in the water. When the stem develops roots, pot up singly into small pots.

November

22

23

Paint fences with a wood preservative now that leaves have fallen and plants do not obstruct them.

24

25

Clean edging-irons, lawn rakes and edging-shears. Wipe bright metal surfaces with an oily cloth.

26

27

28

◄ Harvest winter cabbages as soon as they are firm and mature.

Flowers
Shallowly fork between shrubs, taking care not to damage their roots. Dig up and burn perennial weeds - if their roots are left they will grow again during the following year.

Flowers
Tender shrubs in tubs on patios benefit from a covering of straw or hay during the coldest part of the year. Cold winds soon damage tender leaves. Protect shrubs by inserting five canes into the compost around the tub's edges, tying them at the top, arranging straw or hay around them and securing it with a spiral of string. Remove the covering when the risk of frost damage passes.

Flowers
Place cloches over Christmas Roses (*Heleborus niger*) to protect their flowers from heavy raindrops falling on muddy ground and then splashing on the flowers.

Fruit

Regularly check apples and pears earlier put in a storage shed. Remove those that are showing signs of decay. If left, they encourage other fruits to rot.

Fruit

Before planting new apple trees, check that they are compatible with existing varieties. All apples need pollen from another variety to pollinate them.

Greenhouses

Houseplants with colourful foliage are particularly welcome in autumn and winter. They can be displayed in indoor hanging baskets and are either planted in the container or left in their pots. First, plan the design by arranging the plants on a piece of paper the size and shape of the container.

Indoor hanging baskets bring colour in winter.

Left: The Christmas Rose flowers in winter.

Organic Gardening

Moles eat pests such as leatherjackets, wireworms and millepedes. Although they also eat worms - which are essential to gardens - it is foolish to kill them.

Everlasting flowers to raise from seeds for room decoration in winter

❀ Poppy
   (*Papaver* 'Gigantic Podded')

❀ Scabious
   (*Scabiosa stellata* 'Drumstick')

❀ Statice
   (*Limonium sinuatum*)

November

29

Christmas presents are only a few weeks away, so drop hints about the gardening tools you need!

30

Where young conifers grown as specimen plants have developed two leader shoots, cut out one of them.

Flowers

If the previous summer was hot and many of your plants suffered from lack of water, consider growing drought-resistant plants and mulching the area with shingle or small stones.

Flowers

Keep cyclamen and azaleas tidy by removing dead flowers. With cyclamen, pull off the flower stems intact, but for azaleas just nip off the dead flowers. ▼

Flowers

Bare-rooted trees and shrubs ordered through the mail may arrive when the soil is frozen or waterlogged. They therefore cannot be planted immediately. Either place them in a cool, airy shed or unpack them completely and put the roots in a trench in the garden, covering with soil.

Flowers

Ensure that tubs on patios are raised on three bricks. If directly on the ground, it encourages the tub's base to rot.

Vegetables

Don't be tempted to retain a few potato tubers for replanting next year - they will probably be infected by viruses and therefore will not produce a good crop. Instead, buy fresh seed potatoes, certified free from viruses.

Greenhouses

When planning a greenhouse, position it to receive the maximum light. It should also be sheltered from cold winds. Ensure that the door faces south or west, so that cold winds do not blow directly into it.

Right: A colourful dried-flower arrangement. This display enriches homes in winter, at a time when there is little other colour.

Below: Strawflowers, pretty in gardens during summer and perfect in dried flower arrangements.

Everlasting flowers to raise from seeds for room decoration in winter

❀ Strawflower
(*Helichrysum*)

❀ Statice
(*Limonium aureum*)

❀ Winged Everlasting
(*Ammobium alatum grandiflorum*)

Organic Gardening

Bats are beneficial to gardeners, eating half their own weight of insects at night. Do not interfere with their resting places - it is illegal in Britain.

December

Darkening nights are drawing in
Log fires are lit, the curtains close
Gardens wait for the year to begin
Inside, gardeners warm their toes!

December

1

If the branches of a neighbour's tree extend over your garden you are entitled to cut them off, but legally you are obliged to offer to return them. Before cutting the tree, however, talk to your neighbour to avoid misunderstandings.

2

3

4

Poinsettias flower at Christmas, but once their display is over they are best discarded. ▶

5

6

7

◀ Don't allow azaleas to become dry - keep their compost moist at all times.

Flowers

Evergreen shrubs and climbers with variegated leaves bring welcome colour during winter. Climbers such as the Persian Ivy (*Hedera colchica* 'Dentata Variegata'), Canary Island Ivy (*Hedera canariensis* 'Gloire de Marengo') and

Above: Astilbes are fluffy-flowered perennials.

Flowers
Prune roses at any time from now until early spring. In cold areas it is better to postpone this job until spring.

Lawns
If you are considering buying a new lawn mower, now is the time to look around for bargains. If your lawn is surrounded by flower beds, a roller type is a good buy, whereas if the lawn is edged with stones a hover type is better as it easily rides over stones that may not be level with the lawn's surface.

Vegetables
Plant chicory roots in large pots of sand. Water them and place in a warm, dark position, about 7°C/45°F. Later, shoots develop from their tops.

Fruit
Prune red and white currants from now and until early spring.

Greenhouses
Keep temperatures at a minimum as the cost of heating increases dramatically for each degree rise in warmth. However, do not leave the greenhouse totally closed - ventilation is essential.

Herbaceous perennials with attractive leaves for use in flower arrangements

❀ Astilbe
(*Astilbe x arendsii*)

❀ Bear's Breeches
(*Acanthus mollis*)

❀ Bishop's Hat
(*Epimedium*)

❀ Catmint
(*Nepeta faassennii*)

---

the small-leaved ivy Hedera helix 'Goldheart' attractively clothe walls. Variegated shrubs for borders include many Hollies, the Spotted Laurel (*Aucuba japonica* 'Variegata') and three attractive varieties of *Elaeagnus pungens* 'Maculata', 'Variegata' and 'Dicksonii'.

December

8

9

10

11

Do not walk on soil unnecessarily as it causes compaction and damages its structure.

12

13

14

◀ When calculating the number of fish you can comfortable have in your pond, reckon on about 12mm/½in of fish for every 9 litres/2 gallons of water.

Flowers
Cover tender herbaceous plants with straw to prevent frost damaging their roots.

Flowers
Repair fences, using either angled metal or blocks of wood. Ensure the tops of the posts are either sloped or fitted with caps to protect the end grain from excessive water.

Vegetables
Continue to harvest leeks and parsnips.

Fruit
Inspect stakes supporting fruit trees, as well as posts and wires for cordon fruits. Replace damaged or broken supports.

Fruit
Check the ties on fruit and ornamental trees to ensure they are not broken or strangling the trunks. Either use a piece of hessian sacking folded several times and secured with strong string, or a proprietary plastic tie that can be easily adjusted as the tree grows.

Organic Gardening

Traditionally, in mild areas shallots are planted on the shortest day of the year (21st December) and harvested on the longest (21st June). Most people, however, wait until February before planting them. Leave their necks just above the surface.

Greenhouses

If the greenhouse is empty thoroughly clean it. Use a small piece of bent wire to remove dirt from between the overlaps of glass. Scrub the framework and glass. Thoroughly wash with clean water. Also, scrub the staging. If possible, leave the door and ventilators open for a few days, especially if the weather is very cold.

Right: Lady's Mantle has attractive leaves.

Below: Foam Flowers are superb in gardens, as well as in flower arrangements.

Greenhouses

Keep the glass clean. Dirty glass in winter can reduce the amount of light available to plants by 50 percent.

Herbaceous perennials with attractive leaves for use in flower arrangements

- ❀ Day Lily
  (*Hemerocallis*)

- ❀ Fennel
  (*Foeniculum vulgare*)

- ❀ Foam Flower
  (*Tiarella cordifolia*)

- ❀ Lady's Mantle
  (*Alchemilla mollis*)

Left: Fennel's delicate leaves.

December

15

16

*Christmastide
Comes in like a bride,
With Holly and Ivy clad.*

17

18

When planning to buy a greenhouse,
ensure it has several ventilators. The total
area of ventilators should be at least
20 percent of the floor area.

19

20

When planning a new fence or wall,
check with your local authority to ensure
you do not erect one too high. Usually, in
a front garden it can be 90cm/3ft high, but
in the rear about 1.8m/6ft.

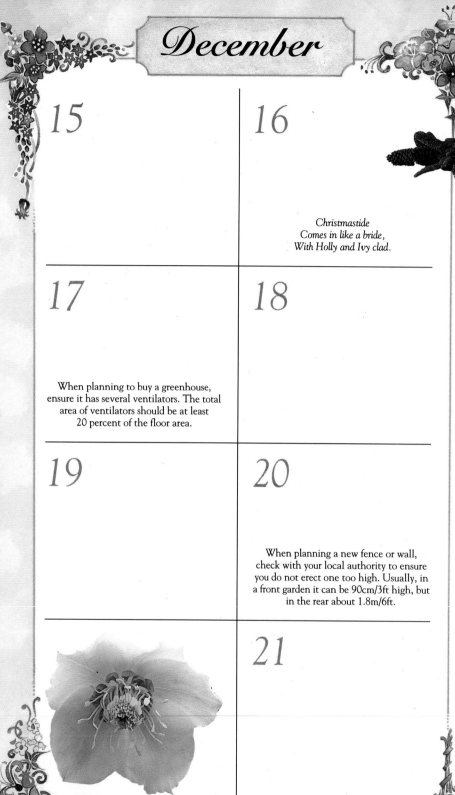

21

Flowers ▲
When cutting evergreen foliage from the
garden for indoor Christmas decorations,
use sharp secateurs and cut to just above
a bud. This ensures that short, unsightly
spurs are not left on a plant. Such stubs
also encourage the onset of decay.

Flowers
The roots of Christmas trees are best
stood in a bucket of water for several
days before the tree is taken indoors.
This helps the tree to retain its needles
and freshness for a longer period.

Lawns ▶
Brush lawns to remove dead grass and
fallen leaves, as well as to scatter
wormcasts. However, if the surface is
wet or frosted, wait until the weather
improves.

Above: A dried-flower basket, which makes a lovely winter present.

Vegetables

Harvest turnips and swedes, carefully lifting them with a garden fork. Remove all soil before taking them indoors.

Fruit

Regularly inspect fruits in store, removing those showing signs of decay.

Greenhouses

Water cyclamen plants carefully, taking care not to wet their leaves and flowers. Pull off dead flowers - complete with their stems.

Herbaceous perennials with attractive leaves for use in flower arrangements

❀ Lamb's Tongue
  (*Stachys byzantina*)

❀ London Pride
  (*Saxifraga x urbium*)

❀ Meadow Rue
  (*Thalictrum*)

❀ Mullien
  (*Verbascum bombyciferum*)

Organic Gardening

If Honey Fungus infests shrub borders, plant resistant types such elaeagnus, holly, mahonia, tamarisk, bamboo, thorn and yew.

December

22

23

*Holly berries shining red,
Mean a long winter, 'tis said.*

24

25

26

27

Brush up the last of the leaves, putting
them on a compost heap.

28

◀ When planting a hedge, do not position
the stems of the plants exactly along the
boundary line. Instead, set them to half of
the hedge's expected width in from the
boundary.

Flowers

Remove leaves from rock gardens. If
left, they retain moisture around plants
and encourage stems and leaves to decay.

Flowers

Re-firm the soil around newly-planted
roses, fruit and ornamental trees and
shrubs. It will be necessary to undertake
this task several times before the arrival
of spring.

Fruit

In areas where rabbits are pests, ensure
that wire netting or plastic guards have
been fitted around trunks. Young trees
are usually the first ones to be attacked
and if totally girdled are killed.

Fruit ▲

Check posts supporting fruit trees. If a
vertical post has rotted away, re-support
the tree with one driven in at an angle of
45 degrees, so that its head crosses the
trunk. The head of the stake should be
into the prevailing wind. Alternatively,
drive two vertical stakes into the ground,
about 30cm/12in on either side of the
tree, and secure a cross support to them
and the tree.

Fruit

When using secateurs, do not strain and
buckle the blades by cutting thick
branches. To cut thick branches, use
either a saw or lopping shears with
long handles.

Organic Gardening

If you have couch grass in your vegetable patch, do not use a rotovator to cultivate the soil as this will chop up the underground stems and make the problem worse.

Greenhouses

Cut down the last of the late-flowering chrysanthemums growing in pots, severing the stems about 15cm/6in above the pots. Remove and burn the stems and leaves, label the plants and keep the compost barely moist.

Greenhouses

Pot up hippeastrum bulbs individually into 13-15cm/5-6in pots, using potting compost. Leave half the bulb exposed, water the compost and place the pot in 13-16°C/55-61°F.

Herbaceous perennials with attractive leaves for use in flower arrangements

❀ Pearl Everlasting
   (*Anaphalis triplinervis*)

❀ Plantain Lily
   (*Hosta*)

❀ Rue
   (*Ruta graveolens* 'Jackman's Blue')

❀ Sea Holly
   (*Eryngium maritimum*)

Above: A Christmas wreath, perfect for a front door where it is able to welcome guests.

Below: Hippeastrum flowers are spectacular and in many colours – white, pink and red.

December

29

30

Before using any chemical in the garden read the instructions carefully - and do not adjust the recommended concentrations.

31

When cutting off large branches from trees, first cut about half-way through from underneath. This prevents the bark tearing downwards when later cut from above.

Below: Winter Sweet, a shrub guaranteed to bring colour and scent to a winter garden.

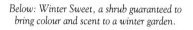

Flowers

Ponds can be given an added quality in evening and at night by the installation of submerged lights and spot-lights. Although lights cannot be fitted until spring, now is the time to dig a trench to take the power cable from the house to the pond. First, however, consult an electrician about its position and depth.

Flowers

Winter-flowering shrubs brighten gardens when there is little other colour in the garden except for variegated evergreen shrubs. Position them where they can be seen from a window, while those with scented flowers are best planted near a path.

Greenhouses

Small, electrically-heated propagation frames are well worth buying for raising plants in late winter and early spring. They enable seeds to be sown in warmth without having to heat the entire greenhouse.

Fruit ▷

If you have an old apple tree, with branches too high for the fruits to be easily picked, it can be topworked. Although this is a little used technique, during winter cut back branches to about 90cm/3ft of the trunk. Pieces of the desired variety are then inserted into the bark around the cuts - three or four on each branch.

Above left: Cornus stolonifera 'Flaviramea' has bright yellow shoots in winter.

Above: Hamamellis mollis 'Pallida' bears eye-catching, lemon-yellow flowers in winter.

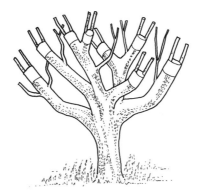

Herbaceous perennials with attractive leaves for use in flower arrangements

❀ Variegated Dead Nettle
 (*Lamium galeobdolon variegatum*)

❀ Variegated Figwort
 (*Scrophularia aquatica* 'Varietata')

❀ White Mugwort
 (*Artemisia lactiflora*)

❀ White Sage
 (*Artemisia ludoviciana*)

❀ Yarrow
 (*Achillea taygetea*)

The Wild Garden

Wild gardens have for many years been mainly formed of azaleas, meconopsis, border primulas and other 'choice' plants from foreign lands. Today, however, the trend is to naturalize native plants in parts of our gardens so that with butterflies and birds they create a real wild garden.

Native plants, so long dismissed because of their common nature, often have just as much eye-appeal as expensive foreign introductions. Seed catalogues abound with native plants, either on their own or in mixtures.

Butterflies can be encouraged by planting wild flowers that appeal to them. Cultivated border plants also encourage their presence and many are suggested earlier in this book, during spring, summer and autumn.

Left: Cowslips (Primula veris) are natives of meadows and pastures. Many seed companies offer seeds of this primula, as well as Wild Primroses (Primula vulgaris). Once established, these primulas will flower for many years.

Wild flowers that attract butterflies and bees

❀ Bird's Foot Trefoil
 (*Lotus corniculatus*)

❀ Bluebell
 (*Endymion non-scriptus*)

❀ Common Toadflax
 (*Linaria vulgaris*)

❀ Field Scabious
 (*Knautia arvensis*)

❀ Heartsease
 (*Viola tricolor*)

❀ Knapweed
 (*Centaurea nigra*)

❀ Lady's Smock
 (*Cardamine pratensis*)

❀ Ox-eye Daisy
 (*Leucanthemum vulgare*)

❀ Purple Loosestrife
 (*Lythrum salicaria*)

❀ Ragged Robin
 (*Lychnis flos-cuculi*)

❀ Soapwort
 (*Saponaria officinalis*)

❀ Wild Thyme
 (*Thymus serpyllum*)

❀ Vervain
 (*Verbena officinal*)

Below: It is easier to establish a large wild flower meadow than one that is small, as it enables larger areas of each species to be grown. The grass creates an attractive backdrop to the flowers. In large wild gardens, create meandering paths by mowing the grass, but take care not to cut other areas until after most of the flowers have flowered and scattered their seeds.

Providing birds with water

Birds need water for both drinking and bathing. Purpose-built bird baths can be bought, but an alternative is to invert an old metal dustbin lid, support it on bricks and fill with water. A nightlight placed underneath in winter prevents total freezing. Do not put salt or antifreeze in the water.

Encouraging garden birds

To many gardeners, birds are an important part of their garden and frequently need encouragement, especially in winter when food and water are difficult to obtain. Fortunately, at least half of all households put out food occasionally and about a third regularly. Food to provide includes:

- Crumbled bread, moistened if dry.

- Bird seed sold in proprietary mixtures. Sunflower seeds appeal to Greenfinches and Chaffinches, while small seeds such as millet attract Finches and Dunnocks (common Hedge Sparrows).

- Stale cake and biscuits.

- Fruit, such as windfalls or bruised apples and pears, appeals to Thrushes, Blackbirds, Fieldfares and Redwings. Dried fruits, such as sultanas and raisins, can be used but first must be soaked in water.

- Cheese, crumbled or grated, is tempting for Robins and Wrens.

- Fat from bacon rinds or chops. Hang from a tree branch.

- Fresh coconut appeals to Tits. Put out pieces of it, perhaps hung from branches. However, do not offer birds desiccated coconut.

- Peanuts, rich in fat, attract Greenfinches, Tits, House Sparrows, Nuthatches, Siskins and Great Spotted Woodpeckers.

- Nuts, crushed or chopped, appeal to Dunnocks and Robins.

Remember ...

- ❀ Don't dead-head plants in autumn as this often removes seeds that birds could eat.

- ❀ Using pesticides kills insects that birds might otherwise eat. Encourage birds into your garden to eat aphids and other pests.

- ❀ In autumn, leave part of your garden untidy, so that birds can rummage through leaves to find food.

- ❀ Thrushes, Dunnocks and Wrens like to feed on the ground, so scatter food on the lawn, but away from bushes where cats may hide.

- ❀ Don't put food on the ground late in the day as it may remain uneaten and could attract rats and mice.

- ❀ Bird tables are relatively safe places for many birds.

- ❀ Seed-eating birds, such as Greenfinches and Chaffinches, have difficultly in finding seeds in early spring, so put out food for them.

- ❀ When the ground is frozen, worms are difficult for Blackbirds, Robins and Thrushes to find, so put out food for them.

Safety and time-saving tips

Using chemicals safely

Chemicals can be safely used indoors and in the garden if a few precautions are taken:

- First, read the label on the bottle or package.

- Double check chemicals used on vegetables, especially the time between spraying and harvesting.

- Do not experiment with concentrations - adhere to those recommended. And do not mix one chemical with another, except when recommended.

- Check that the chemical is right for the plant and the problem it is to control.

- Do not keep any chemical except in its original container - don't put it in containers that appeal to children.

- Store chemicals out of reach of children and pets. And when mixing, keep them away.

- Keep plant-eating animals such as guinea pigs and rabbits off newly-sprayed greenery until it is dry or after it has been cut.

- Avoid contaminating fish ponds, swimming pools and bird baths, as well as fish tanks indoors.

- Take houseplants outdoors and place them in plastic bags to spray them. This ensures that delicate fabrics and wall-papers are not damaged.

- Wash your hands after using garden chemicals.

- If garden chemicals splash in your eyes, seek medical advice immediately, taking the chemical and its packaging (in a plastic bag) with you.

Electrical safety in the garden

Electricity in the garden has made gardening easier and more enjoyable, but it must be treated with respect.

- Never use a piece of equipment that is not connected to the mains supply through a current-breaker (also known as a power breaker) device. This immediately shuts off the power if a piece of equipment is faulty, has frayed cable, or loose connections.

- Have electrical equipment serviced every year by a competent electrician.

- Don't use electrical equipment in the wet.

- Only use cables, sockets and plugs in the garden that are approved for outdoor use.

- Turn off the power at the mains before adjusting any equipment.

The 'unthinking' accidents

Many accidents in gardens appear 'just to happen', but most are avoidable.

- Don't leave tools all over the garden - keep them where you are working. When not in use, push garden forks into the soil, and do not leave rakes so that if stepped on the handle flies up and hits you.

- Wear protective clothing and gloves when using powered equipment.

- Each year, many gardeners lose their sight or have an eye damaged through dust, dirt and wood splinters piercing them. Always use protective goggles when using powered equipment. Also, beware of bending down and the top of a cane or stake poking an eye.

- Wear gloves to protect your hands from dirt, especially when dealing with compost heaps that might have been infected by rats.

Quick tips

Levelling: To assess the general levels in a garden, insert a piece of clear, tubular plastic into each end of a hosepipe, then fill it with water. Secure one end to a short, upright post, with its top at the desired height. The equivalent height is indicated by the water-level at the other end.

Creating flowers beds: Use canes and string to mark out flower beds before cutting them.

Estimating a tree's height: Fix a 1m/3¼ft long piece of wood at 45 degrees to the top of a 1.8m/6ft long pole. Hold the pole upright and look along the angled piece of wood until it aligns with the tree's top. The height of the tree is the distance from the trunk to the pole, plus 1.8m/6ft.

An A to Z of gardening 'phone lines

Bedding plant specialists

....

....

....

Building materials

....

....

Bulb specialists

....

....

Children's swings and garden equipment

....

....

Conservatory manufacturers

....

....

D.I.Y. centres

....

....

Fencing contractors

....

....

Fencing materials and gates

....

....

Fruit trees and bushes

....

....

Furniture and ornaments

....

....

Garden centres

....

....

Garden shed manufacturers

....

....

Garden shed erectors

....

....

Garden tool suppliers

....

....

Glass suppliers

....

....

Grass – contract cutting companies

....

....

Greenhouse manufacturers and suppliers

....

....

Greenhouse plants

....

....

Houseplant specialists

....

....

Landscape designers

....

....

Lawnmowers – servicing and maintenance

....

....

Ornaments for the garden

....

....

Paraffin suppliers

....

....

Patio plants

....

....

....

Patio specialists

....

....

Pots – ornamental

....

....

Rock garden plant specialists

....

....

Seed specialists

....

....

Shrub specialists

....

....

Tools – hire shops

....

....

Tree surgeons

....

....

Turfing services

....

....

Rubbish skip suppliers

....

Water garden specialists

....

....